Anne ...

Thanks

Brian Basilico

REVIEWS

"A powerful book, full of wisdom, yet presented in a joyful, upbeat manner. This book has profound implications for how we can successfully market ourselves and our businesses within the rapid pace of change. A must read."

- **Al Ritter**
  speaker, trainer, author of The 100/0 Principle and Life is a Paradox
  www.ritterconsultinggroup.com

"When we needed a partner to share insights on social media marketing we turned to Brian Basilico. Brian's relationship-building insights are fun, funny and right on target. This book is a must-read for anyone wanting to up their branding, marketing and networking skills!"

- **Rich Kizer & Georganne Bender**
  Speakers, consultants, and consumer anthropologists, authors of Champagne Strategies on a Beer Budget! *and* Jingle Bells, Christmas Sells: Events, Promotions and Tips for the Holiday Season, *co-authored with Australia's Debra Templar.*

  www.kizerandbender.com

"Brian is ahead of the curve with his advice on sorting through the maze of networking avenues to be the one your customers and prospects know, like and trust. He shares why you need to build relationships with people rather than trying to interest and sell to the masses though electronic interaction...and he shows you how to do it. It's a must read for today's entrepreneurs."

- **Lillian D. Bjorseth**
  Speaker, trainer, coach, author of Breakthrough Networking: Building Relationships That Last

  www.duoforce.com

"Communication with people where they are and treating them as human beings is the main message throughout "It's Not About You: It's About Bacon." In fact, there's something for everyone in this book. Whether you're a foodie who loves bacon, an animal-lover, a baseball fan, or a Disney-lover, you'll find a metaphor in this book that speaks directly to you about relationship marketing. That is exactly what makes this book a perfect model for what Brian Basilico explains in this fun, yet packed-solid manual on using social media, marketing and getting results. Highly recommended!"

- **Felicia J. Slattery, M.A., M.Ad.Ed.**
  Speaker and Best-Selling author of 21 Ways to Make Money Speaking and Kill the Elevator Speech: Stop Selling, Start Connecting

  www.feliciaslattery.com

"Brian Basilico is a man I know, like and trust. His new book will teach you exactly what, why and when to use social media. Just as he has taught me over the past 6 years. This book's techniques are proven and steadfast using brain-based technologies that every person uses every day whether they know it or not. Brian will teach you — just as he has taught thousands of others — the magic of using social media to build relationships with your clients or customers, and dispel the myths of creating a brand image and how it actually works.

Relationships are built on knowing, liking and trusting. Brian Basilico and "It's Not About You, It's About Bacon" is incredible. Trust me, you will read it more than once!"

- **Sally Rutledge-Ott, ACE, NFPC**
  President & Founder - Women With Power

  www.srutledgeott.wordpress.com

DEDICATION

This book is dedicated to my best friend and wife Kimberly Joy. You have picked me up when I was down, pushed me when I was slow, put up with years of bad jokes, and corrected my bad grammar in my blogs. You've endured the countless trials and tribulations that have led me to the point of really discovering who I am.

I love you and you make me not only a better person, but a complete one.

ACKNOWLEDGEMENTS

To my mentors Al Ritter, Georgeanne Bender and Rich Kizer: you have taught me how to visualize my ideas, how to convey them, and that politicians give speeches and speakers give presentations.

To my mom and dad, Rose and Harold: I know you are looking down from heaven and smiling that all my gyrations in life led to something constructive and of value to others. You were awesome parents, role models, neighbors and loving members of your community. People today still smile and remember you fondly when I mention your names!

To my reviewers Matt Brennan, Becky Hall, Ellen Huxtable, Jeff Kuczora, and Susan Price. Your feedback really helped me focus, taking this book to another level.

To my book designer Jackson Price. You brought my book to life and gave me a target to write to, and a visual to start conversations and prime the promotion pump.

To my editor Susan Price. I am sure I made you cringe with my "there, their, they're" moments…and those were the easy ones to read, cringe, and repair!

To my indexer/proofreader Lisa Price. You added a level of professionalism and polish that took this project to the next level. Thanks for taking the time to listen and insert your expertise into the book.

To some other important people in my life: Barbara Walter & Bruce Basilico (my sister and brother), uncle Bobbie (RIP) and aunt Tina, my in-laws Dennis and Phyllis Wilkey, my step kids Tiffany & Timmy, friends Rick &

Laura Bursh, and Dave & Julie Locke. And Especially our dog Buddy Guy who gives me 30 minutes a day to think, dream, refocus, and check PMail on our walks!

To all my clients and vendors: You have gifted me with your KNOW, LIKE, and TRUST. We have ventured many roads together, some new and some well-traveled, but we have continued to sharpen each other with patience, perception and perseverance.

And finally...

To you who wish to better yourselves by taking the time to read this book as well as my blogs, podcasts and webinars. You humble me and encourage me to continuing to try to make the world a better place through collaborative education!

I feel blessed that social media have given me the chance to reconnect or stay connected with many people through music, business, or life in general.

TABLE OF CONTENTS

INTRO

And it turns out that tribes, not money, not factories, that can change our world, that can change politics, that can align large numbers of people. Not because you force them to do something against their will. But because they wanted to connect. - Seth Godin

Millions of stories, posts, tweets, and blogs get posted everyday about on-line marketing success. Probably hundreds of millions more stories go untold about people creating successes through face-to-face networking.

What's happening to our business world is nothing short of a revolution. We see change happening at an increasingly rapid pace. We also see people starting to re-embrace the values of the 1950s and '60s. What can't be denied in business is that a customer-centric focus has become more important than ever before in our history.

We no longer can broadcast, advertise and shout ourselves into success anymore. The customers now hold the remote control and can change the channel at will. They can choose to be where we are communicating, or not. We no longer act as the hunter, but must learn to be what they want to hunt.

Customers can make or break us through on-line conversations with their contacts: friends, neighbors, relatives and co-workers. They can choose to comment about your business in multiple forums and on separate platforms, speaking to hundreds, thousands, even millions of people. Are they going to leave a positive review or are they going to take you to task, justifiably or not?

It's up to us to meet customers and potential customers where they are, follow their leads, and create conversations that put them in the forefront of our focus. We need to be accessible like never before. For some of us, that means connecting or being available to them 24/7 and 365 days a year.

Knowing where our would-be customers prowl is just the first half of the social networking process. We also have to use the technologies that they embrace. The responsibility is yours to learn these technologies and adapt them to help your business. And for the process to work, you must learn to communicate in a way that focuses solely on your customers' wants, likes, and needs.

You see, It's Not About You!

It's about your customers interacting with you and your messages. It's about your customers getting what they expect when they interact with you. It's about being top of mind when someone not yet a customer is looking to purchase what you offer. It's about them.

Why read this book?

You probably own a small or mid-sized business. Maybe more than one. You need to learn to look at your business through new lenses, the ones your customers or potential customers see you through. Perception is a business reality, and it's your job to shape and mold a perception that puts you and your business in the most favorable light.

Reading this book should help you understand that you and your personal brand are as important as, and sometimes more important than, your product or service brand. You will realize that it's your job to define and shape that brand through interaction and engagement.

This book should help you embrace the concept of social networking by showing why so many people are talking about it. Also, it will try to debunk the idea that social media are the new frontier in advertising. It will review some of the most common and popular social media platforms, and whether they may or may not be the right tool or choice for you brand and your business. Finally, it will look at how to use social networking to your advantage while avoiding some common pitfalls.

More WHY than HOW

Hundreds, if not thousands of books now exist on social marketing how-to: textbooks, books for dummies, or books on maximizing Facebook, Twitter, LinkedIn and so on. This is not a how-to book, it's more of a "WHY-to" book.

The social networking game is really just getting started, and this book aims to entice you, encourage you, and educate you as to why you and your business must join this game. The goal is not just to be in the conversation, but to learn how to start it and direct it in a way that you will be top of mind when someone needs your product or service.

Just remember... It's Not About You... It's About Bacon!

PART 1:
NET-WORKING IT

Social networking works on three key relationship factors: **know, like and trust.** But it also uses techniques and tools to help you engage with people. What those people (your potential customers) do when they engage with you determines whether you succeed.

Your ultimate goal is enticing people to your home base. We will explore what that means, social networking best practices, and how you can maximize your investment in time to produce their investment in trust!

This process depends on three key factors.

- First, you have to have a solid home base, a place where people find a clear indication of what you want them to do and how they can effectively interact with you.

- Second, you must be able to measure how people get to your home base, and how they interact with you once they get there.

- Third, you'll need to drive more traffic to measure and learn how to create value for those who ultimately get to your home base... your website!

CHAPTER 1: RELATIONSHIP MARKETING

BACON-IZMS

- Marketing has evolved over the decades

- Business used to be all about personalized service

- Technology has changed the game

- Marketing has many meanings and variations

- Social media have revolutionized marketing on a personal level

- Businesses sit at a marketing crossroads

- Relationship marketing is treating people as people

- All networking starts with a smile and a handshake

Marketing has evolved over the decades

I have spent more than 30 years in business. During that time business has experienced many changes, innovations, breakthroughs, revolutions, and upheavals. I've had the chance to see the birth and evolution of the personal computer, and worked at the company that pioneered the cell phone, then watched the "brick" phone transform into a computer that fits in your pocket. I've watched, and evolved with, the growth of the internet. I experienced the world before browsers, email, websites, Google, Facebook, and watched in awe as these new technologies emerged to create a huge paradigm shift in the ways we could, and probably most should, do business.

Business used to be all about personalized service

Before the internet, all business happened in person, by mail or over the phone. People had no eCommerce: no eBay, Amazon, FedEx, or cloud computing. People generally had to walk, use public transportation, or get into their cars to go to a store in person to buy products. To receive services, you might have had the option of ordering by phone or mail, and some products could be ordered for delivery by phone or mail as well.

Back then, relationships were everything. If you shopped in your local downtown, you knew the store owners and they knew you.

One of the first real jobs I ever had was as a shoe salesman at Joe's Shoes in downtown Wheaton, IL. It was a family owned and operated store that was known for two specialties: kids' corrective orthopedic shoes, and women's oversized shoes (sizes 12-15). Those specialties were a big part of Joe's brand and why people came there instead of going to the other shoe stores in town.

We used to keep each client's information on index cards in a box, so when one walked in, we knew what she liked or what that family bought last time. Those cards meant we could provide the customer service that Joe's clients had come to expect. All of that service is what helped people justify paying the premium prices for specialty—and regular—shoes.

Even then, people had many other options: mall stores, K-Mart, Venture, and the other local or chain department stores operating in the area. Those places primarily competed on price.

Back then, business was all about people and relationships. Getting to know the customers on a personal level defined what customer service was all about.

Technology has changed the game

Fast forward to today. We all have data and lots of it. We have databases, contact managers, spreadsheets, accounting systems, analytics and more. Practically everything we do online is being recorded, processed, analyzed, and profiled. Big companies like Google and Facebook probably know more about you and your habits or preferences, than you, your family and friends do. They know what you like, when you sign into your computer, what you search for, roughly where you live and more.

Companies like Zappos (zappos.com, an online clothing retailer) use this data to build a very loyal following of repeat customers who generate a huge buzz via word of mouth advertising. What makes them a standout in the online retailing industry is that to don't view themselves as an eTailer that sells products. They view themselves as a customer service company that delivers products.

It's real easy to get mired down in all the data and technology. We have converted people into channels, avatars, and profiles. We look at buying patterns, categorizing them through graphs and charts, and trying to predict behaviors.

What's missing for all the equations is... people are people.

Marketing has many meanings and variations

Generally speaking, marketing tries to marry customers with what you have to sell. To do that, marketers do **research** to see what people want, and use what they find to **communicate** why people should want what you offer.

Market research helps us determine the best type of customer for our product or service. We look for people in certain economic or business groups. Then we look at buying patterns and try to position our product or service to be accessible and attractive.

Marketing communications include branding, and the creation of messages and advertisements that promote the features and benefits of our offerings. Often these communications seek to differentiate us from our competition.

Internet marketing uses online tools and technologies to deliver our messages to people by means of websites, emails, text messages, tweets, instant messages and more. The internet seems very attractive and useful because it provides a fast, flexible, targetable, and generally less expensive (sometimes almost free) alternative to traditional media such as print radio, and TV.

Social media have revolutionized personal level marketing

Many people view social media websites as excellent internet marketing tools, because they allow you to create conversations and interactions. Social media sites also allow you to create marketing segments where you can promote specific messages to selected audiences.

The intrinsic problem with marketing is that people have to **want** you to market to them for your messages to be accepted, relevant, and acted upon.

Businesses sit at a marketing crossroads

We have come to an unprecedented time in business. Businesses large and small find themselves at a crossroads of marketing tools, principles and methodologies. The biggest change and challenge is that of being effective communicators at a time where the audience gets to control (at least to some degree) the messages they receive.

People can choose to opt in to or opt out of your messages. If you send unsolicited email without giving the user a choice to join in or stop the madness, you may be breaking laws. You will certainly annoy some of the people you are hoping to attract.

People can choose which social networks they belong to, and they control their experiences there. They choose when to log in (or not) and, in most cases, they can and will block or de-friend you if you become an annoyance. The power to connect no longer resides solely in the marketers' hands but is getting more and more user-centric.

All businesses should examine what has worked in the past in light of what is working now. The real trick, though, is to figure out what will still work in the future. Some businesses will choose to stay with their current course, while others will turn on the blinker and make a sharp turn. Either way, you'll need to start asking permission to contact people to get them to listen to your messages about your products and services.

Relationship marketing means treating people as people

Relationship marketing is a mixture of the old ways and the new ways of marketing. It starts by simply treating people like people.

You get to know them on a one-on-one level. Then they give you permission to communicate with them on a social level. Finally, if they get to **know**, **like**, and **trust** you enough (those three key concepts, about which more later), they may buy from you or recommend you to their friends and connections.

If you are a multinational corporation, then you may do all of this on-line, which is how Zappos does customer service. But my guess is that you, like the vast majority of my readers will run a small local or regional business. You are blessed with the opportunity to meet with your customers face to face, just like we did at Joe's Shoes.

You have the opportunity to get to know your customers on a personal level and connect with them in ways that make them feel respected, important and genuinely valued.

If all you care about is making a sale, then you might as well put this book down right now. But if you want to establish highest quality (and often lifelong) relationships with customers, vendors, employees, and the community, then this book will be an enjoyable and fruitful read.

The information that follows will help you understand business through your customers' eyes better. From reading it, I hope you get some perspective on how things have changed over the years, and how the new era of social media can help you start, grow, and nurture relationships.

You will also get some perspective on internet tools and technologies that may or may not be right for you and your business. Ultimately, you will better understand that you're no longer in control (or at least not as much as you used to be). The customer now chooses you, and you have to work harder to convince customers that you are the right choice.

All networking starts with a smile and a handshake

There is no better way to do this in todays' short-attention-span-theater, gigabit-speed, totally connected internet world, than starting with a smile and a handshake.

CHAPTER 2:
CHA CHA CHA CHA
CHANGES

BACON-IZMS

- Communications and Technology change rapidly

- You can't control change, it controls you

- There's a reason for all those free internet tools.

- You can't opt out of the internet

- Advertising runs on volume, of dollars and eyeballs

- Social networking is about relationships

- It's Not About You, it's about people choosing you

Communications and technology change rapidly

Our world is changing at a very rapid pace. Technology advances daily, right before our eyes. Communications devices like computers and phones are getting smaller, faster, and more user friendly. Digital cameras now show up in almost every computing device.

Social networking takes these devices and offers relatively new communication tools that are changing the way we create and manage relationships. Social networking, done well, can give you an incredible tool to help grow your business online.

Chances are, you are in one of two camps: 1) those who embrace technology or 2) those who are overwhelmed with all the change. My goal here is to help you better understand and how to embrace these changes. You will hopefully learn to become a networking superstar. One that people look up to, seek out, and want to do business with!

You may remember the old days (I think it was the 1990s or 2000s). You would go to the store to buy, or have shipped to you, a new program. It came in this thing called a box. On the outside, it would be shrink-wrapped and have beautiful graphics that would tell you of all the features and benefits of this newest and greatest thing that you were about open. You'd take a pen or a knife, and you would find the edge where you could cut the plastic and pull it back to unwrap the glorious golden technological egg you'd just purchased.

The first thing you would need to find was the thing (usually packaged in a small, flat square envelope or box), that delivered the utility of what you purchased: the disc. This disc contained hundreds or thousands of dollars worth of software, which you would take out of its package and load into your floppy, CD or DVD drive to install your brand-new program, or the latest and greatest version of something that you enjoyed, loved, used, and worshiped. (OK, worshiped may be a stretch.)

As the software was loading, you might have gone back to that box to pull out another, larger and heavier gem: the holy grail of information, the installation manual. Well maybe not the Holy Grail but definitely something you needed to make sure that you were doing the installation right.

After the software installed, you'd reach back in that box and pull out another book, the instruction manual. This gave you step-by-step instructions; information not only about what was new with the software, but how to use it to the best of your abilities.

You can't control change, it controls you

Fast forward to today! Now what happens is, all you have to do is turn on your computer. Without you even knowing it sometimes, the latest and greatest versions of software have downloaded to your hard drive. More likely than not you have no idea what's changed. You often find features that you don't recognize, and that menus have moved around from places you expect to find them. No book comes with your updates and nothing that instructs you on how to use the new version or what's changed. Most of the time, there's not even a PDF that explains the difference, or something in the help menu that tells you what's new with version 6.5.3.2.... What you're left with is instantaneous change.

It's up to you to find the company's website, search for the updated program information, and find out what's new. Or maybe you prefer to go to an industry website that gives a quick review of what's changed in your particular program. The onus is no longer on the company to provide the documentation on software updates... It's on you to find them.

Even if you do buy new program out-of-the-box, the cost of printing, shipping, and maintaining inventories of printed materials has made printed manuals history. If you're lucky you get a disk with a few training videos, or a PDF manual. If you tried to print some of these e-manuals, you'd quickly understand why printed documentation is a thing of the past: you might hundreds of dollars in ink toner and paper.

Is this so bad? Well, that depends on how familiar you are with the software, and whether this is just a standard update (to fix holes loopholes or problems) or a serious update to the software (with new features new menus and new options). In this short-attention-span world, you now have to adapt to the rapid pace of change like never before in your career.

The scenario I just described also applies to new media technologies like Facebook, LinkedIn, Twitter, Pinterest, YouTube, and more. Every day, when you log into whatever account that you use, you could find new features: new buttons and other changes made overnight and often without warning. These changes affect your ability to use the software, by changing what tools you have at your fingertips.

When Facebook switched over from its last rendition to 'Timeline', people hated it because they were just getting used to the old way of things. Users thought the old pages worked just fine (even though most didn't like it). But all of a sudden, the whole screen looks different. The information was broken into columns. You now had to create something called a 'timeline cover photo.' All the things that we'd spent months learning were now gone and we had to start all over, learning a whole new metaphor of something that we had just been getting comfortable using.

Then most recently, they changed the layout in your personal profile again. Another new metaphor, another new system, another new way of working with and sharing information. For some of you, change sucks, while for others, it's exciting and you can't wait to get the latest version.

Here lies the intrinsic problem... IT's FREE! We didn't purchase anything. We didn't even install anything. We just signed up and logged in. We certainly don't get the right to dictate the functionality of free software, although some companies may welcome user feedback.

There's a reason for all those free internet tools

Companies like Facebook offer you free functionality in exchange for your use of it, for the rights and abilities to record information about how you use it and what interests you. The social media company uses the information thus aggregated to sell you something. Or it may sell that information to third parties. Why? So that the company can make money! Even though it looks and smells like a free lunch, we are all basically guinea pigs in this world of this new millennium marketing.

Google was the pioneer in this information industry. Google started out as a project by some students at Stanford and incorporated on September 4, 1998. It has since built itself into a $600-$700 per share, publicly traded company. Google owns more than 70% to 80% of the search engine traffic.

This model of giving you something for free so the provider can aggregate data is prevalent across all the websites we currently use for social media. Companies build up a database of what you do, what you like, where you are, what you are doing, and interpolate that against what your friends like, what you search for and where you go on the internet.

People have no problem signing up for this or that web service to explore the latest and greatest free thing. But how long could anyone stay in business if they gave away everything for free without getting something in return? So by giving you all this free stuff, they make the rules.

You can't opt-out of the internet

Some people want nothing to do with Facebook or other social media, but they use Google every day. They think that social media is just an invasion of privacy. They also couldn't care less about what people have for lunch, where they are going, or what awards their kids are getting at school. They don't understand what the big deal is with social networking, and just don't want to use it.

These people don't realize that their train has long since left the depot. Every imaginable detail about your life (except those protected by law, like your credit and medical histories) can be found on the internet: your phone numbers, where you live, what you and your neighbors paid for your houses, and so much more. People who think they can stay private by avoiding Facebook or Twitter only kid themselves. Refusing to look at or use social media sites, or join the social media networking revolution will not protect you or your privacy.

You may feel the warm conviction of knowing, "This is the way it's always worked", and you may feel proud that you resisted the temptation to go where all these crazy people are going. But you only have two choices, either you punch your ticket and ride the train, realizing that you're not in complete control of the destination, or you can stand back and watch everybody else wave goodbye.

I guarantee, as you sit in that train station watching millions of other people of moving forward, you will end up second-guessing yourself.

The people who stubbornly hold onto the past are easy prey for Yellow Page salespeople, who convince them that their customers are just like them and will look for them in a printed book rather than on the internet. They hold onto their beliefs like Don Quixote in Man of La Mancha.

But... no matter how much they want to resist, the rest of the world is forging ahead and leaving them behind. The internet is everywhere... on our computers and our phones, in our coffee shops and cars, and coming soon to our appliances and anything else with a battery or an electric plug (including our electric plugs and light bulbs). You may respect and love the past, but change is not going to stop happening just because you ignore it! In the end, all you are doing is giving yourself permission to be left behind.

After being in business for this many years, the one thing that's sustained my business is my ability to recognize change, embrace it, adapt to it, and realize that reinventing yourself is a far more productive way of staying relevant than rejecting change.

Back in the 1990s, at the height of the digital technology revolution, I built a recording studio business with more than a quarter of a million dollars worth of gear (which I bought $100 or $1,000 at a time). I used the profits to grow my technology, to keep pace with what was happening. I kept growing, striving to be bigger and better.

Today, for less than $1,000, you can buy hardware and software that plugs into your desktop computer. It far exceeds anything my 1990s equipment could have done. It gives higher audio quality and an incredible ease-of-use that I might only have dreamed might be possible 20 years ago. Even more impressive: if you have a smart phone, you can go online and buy an app for between $10 and $99 that will do just as good a job as all that equipment I purchased back then.

So understand that change is going to happen whether we like it or not. Realize that you have a choice: to jump on the social media train, or keep doing what you're doing and hope that you can sustain your business a while longer. Meanwhile, your competition is moving ahead of you.

Advertising runs on volume, of dollars and eyeballs

If you are older or have been in business for a while, then you probably tend to gravitate to what has worked in the past. Advertising has historically been about creating a message about your brand, its features and benefits, while getting to a large audience. All with the hope that the message will resonate with enough people interested in purchasing your products and services. You need to get enough sales volume to justify the expense. Advertising is a form of what marketers call outbound marketing. You broadcast your message to many with the hopes of connecting with a few... your target audience.

A Super Bowl Ad costs upwards of $100,000 per second to air because advertisers can count on upwards of 110 million viewers. So a 30-second commercial costs more than $3 million to air. How insane is that?

Not very, once you do the math of costs versus bene-fits. Say you sell $30,000 cars. If you convert just 1/10th of 1% of those 110 million views to sales, you sell 11,000 cars, totaling $330 million in sales. That equates to about a 110 times return on your investment. Not to mention the brand recognition for other vehicles and service and maintenance. Wikipedia (en.wikipedia.org/wiki/Passenger_vehicles_in_the_United_States, accessed June 3, 2013) reports that, in 2009, about 5.5 million new passenger cars sold in the United States.

Keep in mind, this is just one example. Potato chips, software, and soda do not sell for $30,000 apiece. So how does that price work for the $3 sale? SHEER VOLUME. Small businesses often try to mimic this advertising model on smaller, local or regional levels. And, if I could guarantee you $110 in sales for every $1 personal-brand pen you handed out at meetings or trade shows, you would fill your office with boxes ready to distribute.

Think of it as fishing with a net. You lower the net into the water and troll for a while. When you feel drag from the net slowing down the boat, you pull it back into the boat. You sort through the catch, keep the fish you intended to catch and release the others.

More experienced fisherman know where they can find more of the exact fish they want. They use historical data, maps, and high-tech equipment (fish finders, depth finders and GPS chart-plotters) to catch more fish, and more of the fish they want. That's what profiling, market research and sales techniques can do for marketing. That's why, even before producing ads, some companies use focus groups to determine what works and what doesn't.

You still need to have multiple impressions—lots of eyeballs on your material—before people start to really see and believe your message. That's why you may see the same ad on TV or hear it over and over on the radio. Repetition is how you get your information to stick in the Joe or Jane Public's mind.

Small business owners and solopreneurs rarely have the time or resources to do that kind of repetitive (and often very expensive) advertising. Guerrilla Marketing by Jay Conrad Levinson extols the premise that, as a small business, you can use guerrilla warfare techniques in marketing. His website says "It is a body of unconventional ways of pursuing conventional goals. It is a proven method of achieving profits with minimum money." Don't get me wrong…I read the book and found some very valuable ideas and techniques, but Levinson is still using traditional methods in tactical ways. Times have changed. So much so, that he wrote another book, Guerrilla Social Media Marketing.

Social networking is about relationships

Contrary to some popular beliefs (and some very misguided seminars, webinars and self-proclaimed gurus), Social Media DOES NOT WORK as ADVERTISING! Social networking done well in no way resembles advertising.

OK, both do count impressions. But, where advertising talks to many in hope of selling to a few, social networking talks with a few, with the hope of selling to a few more.

Let me explain. Relationship marketing works by growing relationships, referrals and power partners. It's not about broadcasting and waiting, it's about engaging, reacting and reciprocating: **Inbound** rather than **Outbound** marketing.

Outbound marketing uses the traditional model of broadcasting your messages and hoping people find you. By creating and dispersing messages to the masses, you hope to generate sales. These messages can get sent out by telemarketing, flyers, brochures, newspaper and magazine ads, cable and radio commercials, trade shows and more. Outbound also includes all kinds of giveaways:

koozies, pens, and those cute printed pads known as ad specialties.

Seriously? How much have you ever bought after getting a pen, ruler or visor, no matter how clever the product tie-in? Chances are, many other factors convinced you to purchase from that particular business. You'll much more likely buy from a person who invested time to teach you something, or gave you special attention, or in some other way helped convince you that their product or service was the right choice.

Inbound marketing is a process that helps prospective customers or clients find you. Then, through referrals, testimonials and relationship marketing, those people choose to do business with you because they now KNOW, LIKE, and TRUST you. Getting people to KNOW, LIKE, and TRUST you is a process, but can be so much more fruitful, cost effective and REWARDING than traditional advertising in the long run.

You start by creating a profile and connecting with friends, relatives, high school and college friends, and clients, vendors and more. Next you invest in them. You invest your time, knowledge, feelings, and more time. I know you are asking, "where is the 110% return on my investment?" Well hold on, because I have a bit more to explain and a few more lessons to share with you before you understand the ROI.

It's Not About You, it's about people choosing you

I'm gonna let you in on a little secret: In today's reality, it's not you choosing the customer, advocate, or power partner... they choose you!

What you have to do is find a way to become distinct, memorable, and top-of-mind. This is the power of social networking and social media, getting you to that top-of-mind position and helping you stay there, you just have to learn how to leverage the tools in a way that creates and enhances relationships.

CHAPTER 3:
BABIES, PUPPIES & BACON

BACON-IZMS

- Social media have changed relationships

- Babies are cute

- Puppies are cute

- Know what interests your audience(s)

- Everyone relates to bacon (except maybe vegetarians)

- Feed your audience what interests them

- Know your bacon

Social media have changed relationships

Relationship marketing means giving up your impersonal method of selling at people and learning to connect with people on an interpersonal level. It's about getting to know people and allowing them to know you.

This means that you can't just treat people as numbers or potential sales anymore, you have to treat them as complex human beings. People who like to laugh, and who have family, friends and feelings.

When you connect with people on a personal level, most will reciprocate. This means that you need to be willing to share some information about yourself. It may mean getting outside of your comfort zone. It definitely means that you have to meet people where they are and not just expect them to come to you.

Part of sharing, is giving to people what interests them. This creates commonality and creates conversations. Nothing does that like, babies, puppies and bacon!

Social networking has forever changed the landscape of relationships. We have become a more interactive and connected society. Whether you use a computer or a mobile device, you have access to people and their lives 24/7.

What you share and how often is a reflection of your relationships. There are public messages and private ones. There are personal relationships and business relationships. You get to pick and choose what to communicate and to whom. You also pick and choose how to respond to other posts, on a personal or a business level.

The key point here is communicating. We no longer simply consume information, we are becoming communities of information. We are sharing and caring for others through these new social networking tools.

Social networking is becoming an extension of face-to-face networking. It will never replace it but you can enhance personal relationships by extending a virtual continuation of what happens in person.

Social networking can also have a negative effect on relationships when you only treat people as potential sales. The responsibility to build a relationship lies with you and depends on how you choose to use social media.

So how do you extend and enhance relationships in business? You do it by being you. Connecting with people on an emotional level means showing your feelings and letting others know you have a life beyond your business. You have likes, hobbies, family, friends, pets, kids, passions and more. What can you share to build connections? Did I mention before that you may have to get out of your comfort zone?

So often people think they have nothing in common with others. "So how do I connect with people I really don't know?"

There is an old saying in advertising, "Nothing sells like babies and puppies!" I offer you these three starting points for building and enhancing relationships. The rest is up to you.

Babies are cute

Everyone loves a baby (until you have to change its diaper). Babies are just cute. When someone posts a picture of a baby in an email, or on Facebook, Twitter or other social media, it gets a lot of likes, responses, and comments.

One of the most successful and recurring Super Bowl ads is the E-Trade Baby. He's a talking, technology-savvy and investing baby who is cool, smooth... and did I mention cute? He represents the antithesis of Geiko's "So easy, a caveman could do it" ads. Sitting there looking cute, he conveys that this online trading process is "So easy, a baby could invest better than you do!" even without the "cool dewd" voiceover.

Most everyone I know has kids, had kids who are now grown, or plans to have kids. We can all relate to the kid firsts... tooth, words, crawl, walk, and so on. Then you get the sports activities, dances, graduations and more.

If people are talking about their kids, you can connect by joining in the conversation, or by offering support or advice when it's solicited or appropriate.

Puppies are cute

Many, many movies, and commercials feature cute puppies, dogs and cats, and for good reason. Puppies embody cute also: big-eyed, soft, warm and cuddly (but training them is a whole other ball game). But more than that, people get emotionally attached to their pets. People often treat their pets like family. Families without kids may treat their pets better than family.

People can be very passionate about their pets, and not just dogs and cats, but rabbits, hamsters, ferrets, and more, including reptiles, birds and even fish. Other people love to comment, "like" and interact with pet pictures and posts.

People use social media to rescue and arrange foster care for dogs and cats. A Facebook group I follow, called Lost Dogs Illinois, helps people reunite lost pets with families.

We adopted, and even named, our latest rescue dog through social media. In the summer of 2011 in Chicago, as the temperatures hovered around 100 degrees, someone stole the copper piping from a rooftop air conditioner at a Chicago animal shelter. Our friend Kandra Witkowski, who worked with the animal rescue called A.R.F. (Animal Rescue Foundation), was asked to come to the shelter to help foster some dogs because overcrowding combined with soaring heat posed a major danger for them.

One of the workers took a video of a black lab retrieving a tennis ball over and over, paying no attention to other dogs barking and yelping around him. Kandra sent a Facebook message to my wife Kim saying, "What do you think of this big guy?". Oh... did I mention that he was days away from being euthanized because he was 100 lbs of active dog and deemed unacceptable for most city folk?

A couple of days later, the big guy showed up in our driveway. We met him and immediately fell in love. A week later, after I returned from giving a presentation out of state, Boomer came back, to his forever home. We loved the dog, but his shelter name? Not so much.

That night I posted a picture of him on Facebook, captioned "Name This Dog." We got almost 200 responses. We tallied votes to get the top 5 and then just stared at him. Did he look like a Mac, a Buddy Guy, a Louie, a Bogie or a Lynard? Because he was a black lab from Sweet Home Chicago, he is now Buddy Guy.

Buddy Guy is a Facebook sensation. Every day at 3 p.m., he makes sure I know he has to check his pMail (thanks Georgeanne Bender). I take pictures occasionally (only when he receives and never when he is sending pMail) and post them to Facebook. When I post the pMail pictures, or him sleeping in his bed or chasing a ball, I get likes and comments in bunches.

People love to post pictures of their pets and people love to comment on them. Some pets even have their own social media accounts. (How they type, I have no idea.) So using pet photos is a great way to connect with others.

Know what interests your audience(s)

OK... now you are asking yourself, "Self? What does this have to do with me, my business, networking or even Social Media?" My goal is communicating about me and my business! Guess what? Social media networking or relationship marketing is not just about babies or puppies or Buddy Guy, and It's Not About You. It's about your audience and what interests them. I grant you that not everyone is a parent or an animal lover, but everyone has some topic or activity that interests them. What about sailing, running, cancer, Alzheimer's, Boy Scouts, Girl Scouts, soccer, baseball, football, swimming, dancing, working out, health, wealth, and wellness? It's Not About You... it about what you will post to help you interact with people you don't yet know.

Online or in person, if you want an audience that pays attention to you, you have to create a connection on an EMOTIONAL level, not just a common interest level. Because people love their babies and puppies, pictures about animals, kids, family and the emotions associated with them garner the biggest attention and the most responses in social media.

The sales and marketing comes later, once the connections have been made. I will explain later some of the how, why and metrics of connecting and nurturing relationships. But too many people try to skip this initial contact step, or just refuse to invest enough time to make it work for both parties.

Everyone relates to bacon
(except maybe vegetarians)

You probably read the title of this book and thought, "What's with the Bacon???"

Georganne Bender (the Godmudda of bacon) and Rich Kizer (of KIZER & BENDER Institute of Marketing Strategy) are consumer anthropologists, speakers, authors and consultants. I started working with them in the early 1990s, when they were key players at Fox Retail Group. We have worked together on projects from message–on-hold tapes to training videos. Recently, we linked up again to give joint presentations on social media.

During prep for a presentation we were doing at the Craft & Hobby Conference and Trade Show in Los Angeles, Georganne said, "Watch this!" She then posted a simple hashtag message, #bacon, on Twitter and said, "By the end of this presentation I will have another 10 followers!" She was right.

For some reason, people love anything about bacon. Search #bacon on Twitter? Search bacon on Pinterest? You will find thousands of people and posts and pins about bacon.

So I decided to learn from the bacon sensei and try it on Facebook. I started posting about bacon. Pictures, quotes, goofy stuff and more! What happened? I quickly got new followers and more people commenting on my posts than ever before.

What's even more eye-opening is that, when bacon-related news happens, like "Burger King bacon sundae goes on the menu," 10-12 people post the same story or pictures on my timeline for me. I hardly need to post anything about bacon anymore. People do it for me. People even order me plates of bacon at networking meetings, to pay homage to my ode de Bacon!

Some people comment that they are worried about my health, or that I am obsessed. Others post things like, "Oooo... That looks Yummy!!!" The reactions may be all over the place, but they're consistently active.

Here's my little secret... I like bacon just fine, but eat it less than once a month. If I have my druthers, I order sausage (I suppose neither is that good for you!).

So why is bacon important? Because it's neutral. One truism about social media is, "Go ahead and talk politics or religion, but you will piss off 50% of your audience!" Bacon is the Switzerland of posts, it's neutral, universal and viewed as friendly and comforting.

What bacon has done for me is create a brand. Bacon makes me stand out from the crowd. People see a post or picture about bacon, and they can't wait to share it with me. It does not matter if it's the first time I see it or the 50th time, I acknowledge their contribution and make them feel like I really appreciate them and their efforts (which I sincerely do!).

Feed your audience what interests them

What babies, puppies and bacon do in your social media postings is get people feeling like they have something in common with you. The home run comes when you get them to share your messages with their friends. This extends your reach beyond your 100-500 friends, another concept I will explain more fully later!

All this talk about puppies, babies, bacon and personal branding is about creating a connection, a common thread, a low-stress excuse to just be people and communicate. But, in our short-attention-span world, some of you want to circumvent this step and get to the task at hand... just sell what you have to sell. This happens in both face-to-face and online social networking.

Please, don't fall prey to the attitude of "Let's cut to the chase... are you a prospect or a waste of my time?" Have you ever been on the other side of that equation? It's demeaning, alarming, and just plain rude!

Consider: Would you ever say you just can't wait to log into your Facebook, Twitter, or LinkedIn account because you want to get barraged with "Come to My Event," "We are having a Sale," or "We are better than Brand X because..." posts? People go to Facebook, Twitter or LinkedIn to connect with friends and family, or on Pinterest to learn about or research something, not to be sold something.

It's Not About You... and your networking presence on social media should have nothing to do with your product, service, business. It's just a way to start conversations, and enhance interpersonal communications.

We would all like to be the center of the universe... but whose universe? Hundreds if not thousands of other people may be selling what you have to sell, in your own town or region. Your audience may not be interested in what you are interested in selling right away, but you can get them interested in your baby, your puppy or bacon!

So... know your bacon

The whole bacon theme is just another way of saying "What makes you different?" or "What makes you more like me?"

Your bacon may include: knitting, basketball, crocheting, jewelry making, golf, cooking, running, scrapbooking, youth baseball, biking, favorite books, football, music, soccer, dogs, reenactments, cats, church, marathons, animal rescue, swimming, technology, hiking, triathlons, camping, volunteering, donating, history, preservation, gardening, painting, sculpting, photography... I could go on for days, but I think you get it.

Your bacon can be anything that interests you, your friends and family, classmates, business connections or any other audience, and which is not overtly connected with what you do for a living. You want to pick a conversation starter, a place where you can teach people or learn from them, a connecting point that makes you more, well... human!

Bacon is not political,democratic, republican, or independent. It's not religious, Catholic, Baptist Lutheran, Jewish, Muslim, Buddhist, agnostic or atheist. It's not divisive, pro-gun, anti-abortion, or constitutionality of anything (insert your pro- or anti- side on any issue). Bacon should be tasty but safe: meat candy!

Other than the long-standing (and often greatly exaggerated) divide between dogs and cats, nothing on my list of possible bacon topics polarizes. Rather, your bacon should create a "Kumbayah" feel... a relational human connection. Something in common. Something to talk about and share, or something to learn or teach.

Also, realize that listening is an important part of creating a conversation. Listen twice as hard or as often as you speak! Online, this translates into reading what others have posted before you comment and interact. Then you have earned the right to present your bacon!

CHAPTER 4:
IT'S NOT ABOUT YOU, IT'S ABOUT RELATIONSHIPS

BACON-IZMS

- Business community should be about the common good

- A corporate job once meant a lifetime job

- The internet has brought us closer than ever

- Old advertising models no longer win

- Referrals and recommendations matter

- You have to play the game to change it

- Build new relationships; nurture existing ones

Business community should be about the common good

Being in business means that you belong to a commerce community. You not only have people that you sell to, but you buy from others. If you are like most businesses, you work with service providers: an accountant, insurance agent, lawyer, and probably others. You purchase office supplies, computers and software. If you make products to sell, you buy raw materials or parts, equipment, labeling, packaging and more. You are part of a business eco-system. You have probably formed these relationships through various meetings, conversations and referrals.

Back in the pioneer days, the old West revolved around its towns and settlements. Decades of movies have ensured that most people think of the saloon, bar fights, and gun duels at high noon when they visualize these towns. But despite the movies' evidence, the most important place in town was not the saloon or the sheriff's office or jail, it was the general store.

The general store constituted a cornerstone of the society. It was where you bought essential staple foods for your family and livestock, fixed broken things, bought new things. It helped you sustain life in the wild West. If that store closed, you might have to travel hundreds of miles by horseback or wagon to find another source for the supplies you needed to maintain your life. Because of that, if the storeowner fell sick, people throughout the town would chip in with help. They realized that the general store was more than just a small business, it was integral to the prosperity and wellbeing of the entire community.

If the general store failed, the whole community would suffer, and might even fail itself. It existed not just to sell merchandise but for the common good, which meant that everyone had a vested interest in its success. The store possessed a camaraderie, synergy, community and purpose!

A corporate job once meant a lifetime job

Although corporations date back to the 1600s, the multinational businesses we now think of as corporations grew out of the industrial revolution. Starting in the 1700s, small companies began growing as mechanical processes allowed scale-up of manufacturing. Factories, fabric mills and food-processing plants started adding hundreds and (by the end of the 1800s) thousands of people to run the production lines. This growth continued up to the Stock Market crash of 1929, and started up again with the production needs of World War II.

Corporate growth in the 1950s gave us suburban sprawl, as corporations expanded beyond their urban beginnings. In the 1970s, we began to notice corporations becoming international superpowers. In the 1980s, deregulation let them grow even more. The number of companies employing thousands of people took off. Mergers, acquisitions, liquidations, and consolidations became the norm.

What had been the Horatio Alger dream of the Nineteenth Century, of starting in the mail room and ultimately owning the bank or factory, now had even more scope. How many loyal workers dreamed of climbing the corporate ladder to become CEO of a multinational corporation?

I grew up in that environment. My first real job out of college was working at AT&T's Network Software Center. I was the geek given the task of labeling the components of an entire video studio (more than 1000 wires and 2000 connections). I got that opportunity through networking - meaning my dad had connections. My father, Harold P. Basilico, had worked for the Bell System for more than 40 years. He had become a national training rock star, renowned for his knowledge and teaching abilities, a man who turned the complicated into the easy to understand.

I was taught that you should go to work for a good company because you could work there all your life and retire with a gold watch and a pension. Those days are long gone.

The internet has brought us closer than ever

Flash forward to today. In many ways, social networking and the internet have brought us back to the good old days. It's brought people together just like the general store did to the communities of the Wild West. It's just that the "general store" now covers every continent, hundreds of languages, and all 24 time zones.

The means by which we do business, the structure of our business community has changed. The internet now provides a 24/7 virtual wonderland of shopping and shipping. However, being active in your commerce community will still help you establish relationships that make your product or service the better choice for your customers even though we no longer need to walk into a store in person to purchase most goods and services.

Even thought the advent of the jet airplane made world a lot smaller , it can still take 24 hours to travel from the US to Australia. However, with Skype you can video chat with friends or colleagues "Down Under" 24/7. Through presentations I have given, web-based and in person, I now have Facebook, Twitter, and LinkedIn friends across the globe. I say friends, but they could be clients as well.

The point is that things have changed. Even if your clients sit within one mile of your location, your brand, business and audience are global. You may not want to, or even need to pay attention to that reality, but that's the new world order.

More importantly, grass roots movements are helping the pendulum swing away from the "big box" machine, benefiting the smaller, local entrepreneur. People are becoming fans of the underdog and local business, because the ecosystem of their family and their livelihoods depend on local business. People are asking friends and coworkers, "Do you know a plumber?" or "Where can I buy (this or that) product?" People are turning to social media to ask people they KNOW, LIKE, and TRUST about products and services. You may still shop at a Walmart, but across America, towns and cities that hope to revitalize local downtowns are getting more involved with their chambers of commerce, urging their citizens to "Buy Local" or "Shop Main Street."

Old advertising models no longer win

Many techniques of communicating that worked in the past are becoming less and less relevant. Newspapers have become shadows of their former selves. During their heyday, they showed up at your doorstep with a hundred-page section called the 'Classifieds' which was a huge money maker for them. It listed jobs, garage sales, and lost and found ads. This has been replaced by Monster.com, Yelp, eBay, Craigslist and others. Some internet job sites are now shrinking just like the papers have, because of LinkedIn and other social media websites.

The Yellow Pages served as the most trusted source to find help for your home and business from nearly the beginning of the age of telephones. Google searches have now replaced the books to the point where most people use the Yellow Pages to prop up a table. They use their mobile devices to search for businesses, reviews and advice from friends on which business to use, which is why Google is worth hundreds of dollars a share.

RR Donnelley's Yellow Pages and other print references have tried to re-invent themselves as services like Dex

Knows, the new "Internet Search Engine" or your "Trusted Marketing Department." They may keep changing their name and their spiel, but the bottom line still stands, that they are probably bad for your bottom line.

They claim to buy Google at a discount. Even if that is close to the truth, they sell the same keywords to your competition. Since the highest payer wins, those who just pay Google are winning more!

Mail still works on some fronts, but most people I know walk past their recycle bins on the way back into their house from the mailbox or post office, and most unsolicited print pieces never make it to the kitchen counter.

I am not saying that newspapers, magazines, Yellow Pages and direct mail have become totally irrelevant, but you cannot deny that their influence has declined. Relationships and the internet have taken their place.

Referrals and recommendations matter

Recently 6-10 inches of rain over a day or two flooded our neighborhood, as had happened a couple of years ago. Some basements were spared and some flooded. The difference I noticed this spring came in how we looked for help. A few years ago, people would walk outside or call neighbors to ask for help or recommendations. This time, they started turning to our new neighborhood Facebook group. People were posting "Does anybody know...?" questions and others responded with names and numbers of plumbers and restoration companies within minutes. Who knows how many texts, direct messages, and internet searches occurred during that same span? I walked our dog Buddy Guy that afternoon and saw no fewer than four recovery crews already at work in the neighborhood.

You see, people are always looking for referrals, recommendations, and experiences from people who they KNOW, LIKE and TRUST. It's all about the common good of the community, and in our 24/7 totally networked world, it's easier than ever to get that information from trusted sources.

No longer do people place their trust in the biggest or most colorful ad. People are fast-forwarding through TV commercials on their DVR. They no longer only listen to commercial radio, they are listening to their IPod, Pandora or internet radio sources. Times have changed.

People now turn to those with whom they've had pleasant, successful, cost effective transactions, and who THEY KNOW, LIKE and TRUST. You can no longer guarantee success by out-advertising your competition, although you can try. You can no longer let an unsatisfied customer just go away, because the internet archives complaints forever. You can no longer just rely on your experience and reputation when even newbies can compete on an equal playing field. You have to manage all of the above. Good news for newbies who get it, bad news for the old guard who don't!

You may be making enough from your established business that you haven't worried about the small guys. If you think they don't matter, you have never seen a piranha attack... enough of those small fish nipping at you can bring you down.

I am not trying to be a Debbie Downer, I'm just trying to wake you up to the new landscape of business in the internet age. (You may even want to finish this book now.) Remember, It's Not About You...

Recommendations are the life blood of businesses today. They come in many forms. Online testimonials posted on Yelp, Merchant Circle, FourSquare, and others matter more than you may realize, or want to. Recommendations exchanged face-to-face, (between neighbors, networking business partners, Facebook friends and more) pack more punch than any advertising you could ever do.

It's about the common good. People making sure that their family, friends and neighbors don't get taken advantage of. It's like the old days of the general store, just upgraded to 24/7 and instantaneous!

You have to play the game to change it

It's no longer enough to just have a website. You have to have an INTERACTIVE website. One that creates conversations, spurs commentary, responds to criticism, and enhances the community. No longer can you hide behind a shroud of out-talking or out-advertising your competition, because they are no longer what you need to focus on. It's about the people that you, and they, serve. In this unprecedented period of society, the masses hold that the power.

Look at what happened in Egypt and Iran. Although the governments eventually seized control again, the cat is out of the bag. The very existence of Twitter, Facebook, YouTube and the internet in general changes things. Information gets shared at a rapid pace. You can say it ain't so, turn away or try to squelch it, but that info-sharing is not going away. In fact, it's spreading much faster than you can stuff that cat back into the bag!

Being an ostrich and putting your head in the sand will not help either. Whether you like it or not, people are going to post about you and your business. Some of it could help you, while other posts could hurt. Either way, you have to come to grips with that, so you can manage it!

I've had clients who call, wanting to try to remove negative content about them from the internet. I have to inform them that the only way realistic and cost-effective way to counteract negative information is flood it out with positive information, pushing it further and further down in Google searches!

Build new relationships; nurture existing ones

So what's a business to do? Build and grow relationships. And remember that new clients are not the only ones you need relationships with. New clients, past clients - and people you may never do business with - not to mention your employees, suppliers, and vendors - can and will all be significant people for your business.

In this ever-changing digital, spreadsheet, Quickbooks report, analytics world, PEOPLE MATTER! Relationships matter. People look very different in person than they do as entries on an income statement.

As a businessperson, you are part of a much bigger picture. Nurturing current relationships and planting new ones is more important than ever before!

CHAPTER 5:
HITTING SINGLES,
DOUBLES & TRIPLES

BACON-IZMS

- Social Networking is about the message, not tools

- You will always hit more singles than triples

- Start with face-to-face networking

Social Networking: it's about the message, not the tools

I was giving a presentation to a local Rotary group. They wanted to know about this thing called Social Networking. If you are not familiar with Rotary Clubs, they are an international service club whose stated purpose is to bring together business and professional leaders with to serve the community.

Many of the members are retired or elderly, so this Social Networking thingy (including smartphones, iPads, texting and more) was mostly foreign to them. I was full of piss and vinegar and I was going to show them what Social Media was, and why it was important to THEM!

I had a killer presentation, with images, graphs, moving slides, statistics, which I thought would make them swoon and help them understand why social media is so important if they want to connect with the world outside of their little group!

I finished a compact but complete 15-minute presentation. When I got to the last slide with my contact information, I was ready and poised for the barrage of well-intended and informed questions that I expected this riveting and informative killer presentation to inspire.

Then I asked, "Are there any questions?" Silence. I stood there for a minute, thinking to myself, "Wow! Do they all totally understand social networking thanks to my excellent presentation?" I was ready to turn around, pack up and leave in glory, when a hand sheepishly rose up from the crowd. It belonged to a 70-something gentleman who asked the hardest one-word question that I've ever faced, "Why?"

I talked around the subject for a few minutes but never really gave an answer that completely satisfied him or the group.

A little while later, I got something that most people only hope and wish for, a second chance to present to the same group. This time, I was bound and determined to convince them that they needed to understand social networking.

I came up with a metaphor that I knew they could relate: baseball. I said that Facebook (family and friends) was first base; LinkedIn (business and work) was second base; and Twitter (the world) was third base. If you loaded up the bases, then you could hit the social media Grand Slam!

At the end of the second presentation, I got a standing ovation. I hit it out of the park: they got it. They understood that Facebook, LinkedIn and Twitter were tools to get your messages out to the masses. But I left the group asking the same question they'd asked me, Why? I'd really never answered that question from the first presentation.

Then I had another epiphany. Those three bases and the home run was the right metaphor, but I'd had the wrong emphasis. It was not about the platforms or the technologies, it was about the Why. Just talking to people on Facebook, LinkedIn, Twitter, YouTube, Pinterest, Delicious, Reddit, StumbleUpon, Technorati, Google Plus or any other platform is not the point, for retirees or for your business. It's about relationship-building:

- First base: people need to KNOW you

- Second base: get people who KNOW you to LIKE you

- Third base: people who KNOW and LIKE learn to TRUST you

That's what I'd learned in books like Duct Tape Marketing, In Search of Excellence, or The Purple Cow, and from authors like Seth Godin, Chris Brogan, Napoleon Hill, Tony Robbins, Peter Drucker, Tom Peters, and more. It's Not About You... It's about getting people to KNOW, LIKE, and TRUST you.

You can get to first base... get people to know you. You can hit a double and get people to like you. You can hit a triple and get people to trust you. But you cannot get to third without touching first and second base on the way, otherwise (just as in baseball) you WILL be called out.

You can't expect someone to like you if they don't know you. And you certainly can't expect anyone to trust you if they don't first know and like you. But some people get up to the plate and always swing for the fences... trying to hit that home run—a sale—with every swing.

In baseball, players hit singles about 70% of the time. About 20% of hits are doubles, and just 2% are triples. Home runs account for only 8% of all hits across major league baseball. Take these baseball facts to heart in your business planning: make those singles count! Getting people to KNOW, LIKE and TRUST you is an investment in an essential process.

If you meet 100 new people networking, you can expect to see 70% of them again if you and they are actively networking face to face. If you can engage 20% of them on a regular basis, 2% of them may turn into regular customers. But relationship marketing helps you increase those 20% and 2% ratios. More importantly, you may convert that 2% exponentially, when those new customers tell their networks about you and your products or services.

Even though I took my example percentages from the baseball metaphor, I see pretty close to those engagement ratios in my business experience. Your actual results will vary depending on your activity, product or service, and frequency at which people need or purchase them.

In the next few chapters I will examine the KNOW, LIKE and TRUST process in more detail. So prepare to Play Ball!

CHAPTER 6:
GETTING TO KNOW YOU...

BACON-IZMS

- Networking beats not working

- Invest the time to become a resource

- B2B is really P2P

- Listen twice as much as you speak

- Growing good relationships takes time

- Quality networking takes time and commitment

- Join strong networking groups with strong leaders

Networking Beats Not Working

Networking, one of the most powerful tools in a business arsenal, requires you to get out and meet people. For some of you, this may be uncomfortable. But it's a necessary part of the relational marketing that will bring you success.

In the last chapter, we learned that getting people to KNOW, LIKE and TRUST you is like getting to first, second, and third bases in baseball. So let's explore first base. (And please, check you adolescent humor at the door—This Is Business!)

I belong to leads groups, networking groups, and think tanks (business brainstorming groups). Add to that volunteering for boards and committees, then tack on two to five opportunities per month to do presentations or teach a class. That all adds up to dozens of hours— almost a full work week a month—spent on something besides working on my consulting assignments.

I know it sounds insane for a solopreneur to spend that much time not directly earning income, but it's time well spent:

- I get to reconnect with those I already KNOW, LIKE and TRUST

- I meet new people who will eventually KNOW, LIKE and TRUST me and my business!

Invest the time to become a resource

I often hear "You are everywhere?" and "When do you find time to work?" Trust me... I pick and choose events wisely and with purpose.

- I want to connect with people who I feel I can help first, and then those who can help me!

- I go into networking expecting to help connect others first, not how can I create more sales.

If you are going to be seen as an asset to people and their businesses, you have to become a resource first, and a vendor second. Yes... I am asking you to forget about yourself, your business and your needs, to become a trusted resource first. Trust me, the business will roll in later!

B2B is really P2P

One of the best philosophies I have ever learned about networking is that business is not B2B... (business to business); it's P2P (person to person). People do business with people, their knowledge, experience and expertise, not their businesses. Businesses are not people, they are organizations by which people to translate their schooling, training, knowledge, and trials and tribulations into products or services that best suit a customer's (or potential customer's) needs, wants and desires, at the time and place of the customer's choosing!

Social networking is an extension of your face-to-face networking. To be successful, you have to master the face-to-face part before the social networking part will work for you.

Listen twice as much as you speak

You may have heard, seen or read dozens of philosophies on face–to-face networking. I want to offer you a piece of advice from other networking experts: God gave you two ears and one mouth... so listen twice as much as you talk!

The worst thing you can do is constantly talk about yourself. Say you see a well-dressed and fairly attractive person and walk up to say "Hi!" You introduce yourself and he or she does the same. And then your new acquaintance dos nothing but talk tirelessly about his or her self, business, products, services, and so on... and on and on. After only a few minutes of these ramblings, you finally get a word in edgewise to talk about yourself only to get, "That's nice, but..." and a continuation of the previous monologue in response.

You listen for a few more minutes before disengaging with a polite "nice to meet you." So what happens when your new acquaintance hands you a business card and asks, "Can I call you? Meet you for coffee? Can I come to your office?" You may politely say "sure," but you walk away saying to yourself, "Damn... I'd thought I'd never get away!" Well, you did but maybe only for a few minutes. When you start talking with someone else, next thing you know, he or she has used your previous conversation to barge into this conversation and started the process all over again, with two victims this time.

You could never imagine being that annoying... but that's the way some people treat social media. Once they get your information, they become pit bulls that refuse to let go. God forbid they ever win a small success (or even imagine one) with this tactic. Once they taste blood, they bite harder and faster, not realizing the damage they are doing. You have all seen people who post every-where, every day, trying to sell the same crap again and again, by putting perfume on it or constantly trying to repackage it until it starts to generate more sales.

Another networking faux pas (French phrase meaning taking a false step in this social dance) is letting poten-tially good contacts slip through your hands. You meet people and have nice, congenial conversations, shake hands and trade business cards. You leave saying to yourself, I'd like to know more about these people and connect with them soon. Meanwhile, they've put your business card on a pile of other cards, where it sits... and sits... and sits. Three months later, these contacts look at your card and think, "It's been so long, this person won't remember me or my business. At best, your card stays in the pile, but most likely it gets tossed into the recycle bin.

Face it... we all get busy, but why would you network unless you expect to get something from it, something like new business, or a connection that could lead to new business. You can't imagine yourself being that passive. You have an address book, tickler file, email list… and you follow up with people you meet at networking events.

However, some people treat social media like that pile of neglected business cards. They post once and expect the whole world to come knocking on their door. Put yourself in the other person's shoes. They know you, they may even like what you posted, but that's not enough for a decision to do business with you.

You probably didn't marry your wife or husband after only one date (if you did, then I apologize). Marriage grows from dating, courting, and meeting the parents, the siblings and maybe even the kids. You take time to get to know each other, and each of your quirks, until something eventually makes you realize you've fallen in love.

But for some reason (maybe it was all those business books about kissing frogs or closing sales), we think that in business we can have one meeting and achieve the greatest sales and wealth ever.

Relationships are hard, time-consuming and work! But GOOD relationships are worth their weight in gold, or more. I have clients I've been doing business for 20+ years. They have followed me through all the changes of my life and career, when I have run my own businesses and when I worked for corporations or small companies. They have followed me and I have followed them. The thing that we have realized is that we are in it for the long haul, through thick and thin, and we have each other's best interests in mind.

Growing good relationships take time

As I stated earlier, each month I spend upwards of 20 hours (half of a normal week) investing (notice the word invest) in first-base networking activities.

Networking means you have to get out of your office (and your comfort zone) and go meet people. You can find dozens of free and paid-for networking opportunities right under your nose. Join a chamber of commerce or an industry group at which you can get out and reconnect or meet new people. Check out meetup.com for dozens (if not hundreds) of meetings in your area. You should also check out BNI (Business Networking International.

I'm sure you get the point by now that networking on a local (and even national) basis can help you grow your business. But to really get value out of it, you have to first ask yourself a couple of questions:

- What are my expectations?"

- What defines a good networking group?

- What constitutes success?

- When do I say enough is enough?

There are no easy answers to any of these questions. In marketing, I like to teach my customers to consider the 3 to 1 rule. If you spend $100 on marketing, you should make $300 total in return... $100 to pay for my services, $100 for your time and expenses, and $100 in profit beyond that. If you spend 1 hour networking, could you sell 3 hours of your time? Or an equivalent value of products?

If you walk into every networking event expecting immediate results according to this equation, I guarantee you will be disappointed. It may take weeks, months, or even years to get people to KNOW, LIKE and TRUST you.

Think of it this way: If you walked into a bank, deposited $100 and came back a week later asking for $300, you would be arrested for attempted robbery (or at least get some looks indicating you were acting crazy). It would take a year at today's 1% interest rates to make $1, let alone $200.

If your product or service is worth $1000, it may take weeks to make your first sale. Then if you sell 3 total (gizmos or hours), you make $3000. Once you start to create a buzz and get some referrals and recommendations, this could balloon to five times the sales. So, let's say you invested 50 hours (an hour a week for 50 weeks) over the course of a year and created $15,000 in sales. Depending on your hourly pay, you would probably consider that a successful investment in time. (If not, then you may be in the wrong networking group.)

Quality networking takes time and commitment

Networking is an investment. It takes time and measurement of results. So often, I see people expecting too much too quickly. They jump in, make their sales pitch and stick around a few weeks or months, but then leave. They may have had a few early sales, but not enough (they think) to support the time they've invested. The real return comes with more time, however. Yes, those weeks or months, or even years, have eaten a lot of your time and effort, but people can take that long to get from first base (know) to third base (trust). They may know and ultimately like you after a few meetings, but by stopping there, you lose the ability to earn referrals because they trust you, even if they've never bought anything from you themselves.

Join strong networking groups with strong leaders

When choosing networking groups, look for groups with the three main factors help define an excellent networking group:

- accountability

- strong leadership

- actively promoting business between members with tons of leads and closed sales.

I belong to and run such groups and can tell you through experience that it takes commitment and a professional team to make networking groups successful for all.

One example of this type of group is 'The Motivated Connection'- themotivatedconnection.com. The brain child of realtor Nicole Tudisco, It is industry exclusive (meaning that only one mortgage broker or one land-scaper, for instance, can be a part of the group at a given time). When a person leaves, members can bring a guest to fill that industry's open slot. It took me years to get into this group because someone in my field was already attending. Once I was invited to join, I learned a lot about what makes a killer networking group tick.

The first key factor is accountability. People are assessed incremental amounts of points for actions that benefit the group, such as those listed here:

- closed business (business between members)

- referrals (another member pointing you out to someone with an immediate need for your product or services)

- leads (a potential business contact)

- testimonials (both in person and on-line)

- one-on-ones (personal meetings with members)

- attending business events run or supported by the group

- bringing qualified visitors

- having your guest(s) join the group

Members who do not accumulate enough points in a quarter or miss too many meetings can be forced to pay a fine or leave the group.

Another factor that makes this group work is strong leadership, an active and committed board of directors, well defined rules, strict enforcement of these rules, compassion, dedication, and members who are reminded to be committed to the betterment of the group as a whole.

The Motivated Connection also holds quarterly mixers where people can just be people and get to know each other on a personal level, not just as another business.

Finally, and most importantly, the best groups have a core mix of people intrinsically linked together by what they do. A group can have 30 people, but no core group of people creates business for each other, then the group has a flaw. Without a core group of people who feed each other business, is the group has no expendable cash to help you and your business. It does not matter whether you are an artist or a multi-level marketer, a group that has no money to spend on existing members has no money for your services either!

What makes The Motivated Connection group tick is a core membership that includes a home contractor, landscaping service, carpet installer, cabinet installer, plumber, hardwood floor refinisher, interior designer, disaster recovery service, and handyman. To that, add a realtor, mortgage broker, and insurance person. These people generate so much business for and with each other that they provide additional business opportunities for other personal and business services. They also make an incredible referral source. This creates a centrifugal force of business that has helped this group expand into multiple groups throughout the area. I have seen, and been to, many networking groups, but this one is a model for networking success for your business!

When considering the many paid-for or free groups out there, try to confirm through observation or personal contacts that the group is generating business for most of its members. Some networking groups are all about creating income for that group's organizer or business. Even some (by no means all) chambers of commerce worry more about sustaining the chamber than promoting business. If you can't confirm benefit to group members… move on! Trust me: I have bought the appealing sales pitches, and I've spent way too much time figuring that out! Ultimately, It's Not About You, but about what others do that creates business around you, and about how you can serve them and help them to create more. So get out there and start making some awesome connections!

CHAPTER 7:
YOU REALLY LIKE ME?

BACON-IZMS

- Getting people to LIKE you takes time and effort

- Looking for relationships, or one-night stands?

- Find success even connecting only to your top 100 people

- You can't buy your way to fans or friends

- Use multiple media to connect

- Your content should create interactions and conversations

Getting people to LIKE you takes time and effort

People may get to know you through networking, but getting people to LIKE you takes more and different time and effort. People only like those will with whom they connect on a different level, of common interests, or commenting on and sharing their passions on social media posts.

You encourage people to LIKE you by becoming a bit more vulnerable, by being more of a person and less of a business rep or a salesperson. You have to be willing to share a bit of your true self: your hobbies, your past, and perhaps your vision for the future. You need to connect with people on a human and emotional level to hope to connect later on a business level.

Looking back, I see how all my experiences have helped me learn how to fit in, be me, and connect with a wide array of people. Those lessons have helped me to better understand how and why networking is key to growing my (and your) business!

Looking for relationships or one-night stands?

I learned long ago (and have understood better more recently) that relationships take time to nurture. Too often, people treat networking events as floating sales meetings, committing for a couple of meetings or a few months, just long enough to get their names and businesses out there.

If you have watched the TV show How I Met Your Mother, you know Barney Stinson. His goal in life is to score as many one-night-stands as humanly possible. He is transactional, all about the deal of the day. He has no scruples and wants nothing to do with commitment. He just wants to "make the sale" and move on to the next conquest. Some people (especially those in commission-based sales or multilevel marketing) treat networking that way. They treat people they meet as mere transactions. They are more concerned about making a sale than a relationship.

Then you have people who want to be more relational, like Carl and Ellie from the movie Up. Up unfolds a love story and a friendship that both extol commitment, dedication, and selflessness! That's how other (and more successful) people treat networking. To network well takes commitment and the knowledge that caring for others can lead to good things.

The Carls and Ellies of this world try to find opportunities to make other people successful. They recommend their contacts when they know people are looking for products and services. They support their contacts, lending an ear or a hand, and do their selfless best to make themselves valuable: to be good friends. the Carls and Ellies use a difficult and unconventional approach, but it works in their favor. By giving of yourself, you become not only a trusted advisor but a friend and, more often than not, those you help will return the favor. Trust me, people can smell the difference between sincerity and scheming!

A huge gap still yawns between a soul mate and a sale, but the closer you get to being a soul mate, the more likely you will eventually earn a customer or client for life! Not every client or customer has to be a soul mate, and some may drift between mere sale and soul mate over time. Either way, I guarantee you that sales are transactions, but soul mates are transforming.

That's what networking is all about... It's speed dating for business. Are you looking for a one–night-stand or a long-term relationship? If the latter, stop fooling yourself and treat your networking seriously.

Now admit it: You can tell the difference between the Barney Stinsons and the Carls & Ellies on your social media.

The Barney Stinsons do nothing to connect with you on a personal level. They disguise ads as caring posts. They never comment on your heartfelt thoughts or issues or offer support and advice. They just post about what they have to sell.

The Carls & Ellies, on the other hand, offer comfort, advice, and connections. They interact with you on a more personal and emotional level, while expecting little or nothing in return.

You meet both transactional Barney Stinsons and selflessly caring Carls and Ellies in your everyday life. Think about the people who serve you coffee, in a national chain or a local cafe. Who takes time to get to know you and your likes? Or the difference between the person at the corner grocery store (who knows your name, the kids' names and how many pets you have) and the WalMart checkout person who wasn't there last month and may not still be there when you come back in a couple of weeks. Who pays more attention to you? And are you willing to pay more for that level of service?

I realize I cannot be there for everyone even as a mid-level player with more than 5000 connections, but, I do my best to engage with as many people as I can, while still getting the work done for clients who need my services!

Social media tools like Facebook, Twitter, and LinkedIn give you the opportunity to nurture the relationships you start in face-to-face networking. Are you treating those contacts more like a Carl or Ellie would, or like a Barney Stinson? Social media activity can build your relationships, or you can be using them to reach for that transactional, one-night stand. Which are you doing?

I have learned that you never know which acquaintance will be the most important connection for your next success, or when that contact will happen! You have to be willing to connect with a wide variety of people in various businesses. You may never make a sale to many of them, but you may connect in ways that help both of you even when they don't necessarily mean direct business. Sometimes, those connections can lead to opportunities that ultimately grow into a successful business!

Find success even connecting only to your top 100 people

So you've joined social networks. Maybe you're just getting started or maybe you've been on them for a while. So what should you be doing?

- Getting more friends and likes?

- Making as many connections as possible?

- Trying to promote more?

No, you need to examine where you are and make a plan to get useful, relational results.

I have participated in way too many webinars that try to make you think that social media is a gold mine, which if you can dig into it, will make you make millions of dollars. Some will tell you that more than a billion people are just waiting to hear from you and give you their money. In their pitch to sell you their $5,000 program discounted to $999 and back-loaded with "But wait, there's more" offers, they never tell you the reality.

First of all, if you're selling in the US, the population totals 300 million or so, not a billion. Subtract the one-year olds and the 90-somethings (or more realistically, the people who don't have access to a computer) and you cut that by a third: say 200 million. Because you can't expect every person who has a computer to be on Facebook, cut that in half, and now you have maybe 100 million people. That's right, one tenth of the audience you've been promised by that smooth-talking salesperson.

Next you have to make the broad assumption that all of those 100 million people need and use your product or service. If you're selling toothpaste, toilet paper or something that everyone uses, OK. Otherwise you have to start whittling away at that 100 million. If you sell to a local audience rather than nationally, your audience shrinks exponentially. In the Chicago area (where I live), the potential audience stacks up at about 10 million. Working with and for other business owners as I do,, my potential audience comes to about 1/10 of 1 percent of that total, or maybe 10,000 people.

Now granted, my target audience is way smaller than one billion people, but 10,000 is still a pretty big number. If I could capture another 1-2% of that annually, I could get 100-200 new customers every year. That translates to a new customer every two to three days, pretty close to what I actually see.

You may have a completely different ratio. Maybe you serve a national audience. Maybe your audience locally is much bigger than just 10,000 business owners, more like one million home owners. Maybe you do have a globally marketable product or service (but you had better be able to cater to multiple languages and currencies and delivery routes before you plan to go global). But the idea of focusing on just the customers you want remains useful.

Take these basic Social Networking numbers to ponder and discuss. Most people on Facebook or LinkedIn or Twitter have around 300 followers. Most business pages on Facebook average 150 likes. Based on those millions and billions mentioned before, this sounds pretty dismal and like a waste of time right? WRONG!

I had a lightning-in-a-bottle experience of a simple post going viral. My two-man acoustic band called Dough! Has a Facebook page. On it, I posted a simple joke graphic about a church choir made of wrenches singing "Amazing Grease, How Sweet the Sound that Saved a Wrench Like Me!" That simple little joke got shared more than 1000 times and was seen by more than 100,000 people. Now my band has only 300+ fans, so how could that happen? (I know, math hurts my brain too.)

Well, if only 10% of my 300 fans shared and 10% of their 300-ish each friends shared the same graphic, that adds up to about 1,000 shares. You only need 100 people looking at each of those shares to get 100,000 views. The bottom line is, social media posts can be shared and thus have the potential of going viral. That's why your 150 fans can give your messages the potential to reach a much larger audience than any postcard or flyer could ever hope to.

You can't buy your way to fans or friends

Use multiple media to connect

So now that you understand how powerful social networking can be, how can you make it work for you? Well, that depends on your audience and the social media preferences of its members. If you get business cards with social media links, it's much easier. If not, then you have to do some detective work.

If you're connecting with business–to-business persons, you may want to search them out on LinkedIn. If your contacts are business to consumer, you may have better luck finding them on Facebook or Pinterest. What tool you use is not as important at this point as what you do with it. I will give some examples in Chapters 19-24 on the uses and advantages of certain social networking tools.

Your content should create interactions and conversations

What matters first and foremost is that you connect and keep in touch with your audience on various levels. You have to connect on a personal level so potential customers get to know you as a person and not just as representing your business. You may meet these people at various networking or business events. Maybe you connect with them on social media on a fairly regular basis. You might see and interact with posts about their family, your pets, your hobbies or other, mutual activities and interests. For some of you, this might feel uncomfortable. Most people don't want their personal lives splattered all over the internet, true, but small doses of your personality and milestones, shared tactfully, can go miles in creating connections.

When "likes" or "fans" see that you are part of Kiwanis or the Rotary, or serve on a nonprofit board, you build credibility. If you coach a youth league or your child takes part in gymnastics or martial arts, that can create another connection. If you mention selling at or going to craft shows, or playing in a musical group, you may find another type of connection.

If all you do on social media is talk about your product or service, you will be considered noise and either ignored or, even worse, blocked or de-friended. Social media is not advertising, but people continue to treat it that way. That is a sure-fire way to fail. Remember, you are trying to get people who KNOW you to LIKE you. That means that you have to focus on them and what interests them, to encourage them to connect with you on a personal level

If you do have a business page or want to focus on business posting, then you have to provide current and

potential customers with interesting, educational information, posts that will keep them entertained, informed, and
interested in what you have to say with your next posts.
That means you have to invest in finding and/or creating
useful content. I will talk more about finding and creating
content in Chapter 25.

Ultimately, having met someone is a first step in getting
them to like you. Once they do like you, you become
top of mind. But if they know ten people who do what
you do, you want to advance to the coveted position of
trusted source. We'll cover that goal next.

CHAPTER 8: TRUST ME...

BACON-IZMS

- Trust must be earned

- Trust can operate one-on-one or between group members

- Exceeding expectations brings referrals

- Create a value proposition that people can trust

- Testimonials and recommendations are golden

- Don't forget to ask

Trust must be earned

Trust is one of the hardest things to earn and manage. Integrity and customer service must be innate in you and your business before you can hope to earn trust. Trust is not something you can buy, negotiate, or circumvent. It has to be earned. Once earned, it has to be nurtured, maintained and re-earned with every transaction, interaction, and reaction.

So, while you may have lots of people who KNOW you, and many may even LIKE you after a certain amount of time, getting them to TRUST YOU... takes even more time, more communication, and usually some direct personal interaction.

You generally earn trust through two distinct pathways. First, you can meet or exceed expectations for a predefined task while working with or for a group, or an individual. Or, you may find potential trust offered to you through referrals, testimonials, or some other happy consequence of someone's first-hand experience with you, and your products or services.

Earn trust one-on-one or between group members

Giving clients over–and-above customer service is a sure-fire way to create a revved-up referral machine. When you exceed expectations, you help clients realize the true value proposition you offer. People who've experienced that commitment to service rush to share your contact information when somebody asks "Do you know anybody who can..."

When you win the opportunity to work with clients, your level of commitment to the project will make or break your reputation. A happy customer can become a cheerleader for your business, rewarding you by recommending you and your business to others. On the flip side, an unhappy customer can spread the bad word like wildfire, especially on social media.

Large corporations have teams of people on staff or on call to monitor social media for negative posts so they can deal with them, responding before the damage spins out of control.

So one of the first things you should do is, be honest with yourself.

- Is this client a good fit?

- Can you meet or exceed their expectations?

- Is this the kind of business that will produce lasting results and referrals?

- Or is it just an opportunity to make more money?

I have found out, more than once, that someone who comes to you complaining about their last vendor or service provider will likely to do the same with you. Some people's expectations are just out of line with reality. Watch out that you don't become just another in a long line of people who cannot satisfy these folks. You can spend way too much time and money, both in trying to satisfy them or collect from them, and in dealing with the negative fallout.

Sometimes, though, people have just been taken advantage of. For them, you really can become their knight in shining armor or Seal Team 6. You have to evaluate each new client or customer on a case-by-case basis. Watch out for telltale signs of future problems, such as when they immediately start asking for lower quotes or discounts as soon as they get your quote or estimate.

If people devalue your knowledge and experience before you even start a job, you are more likely to experience something called "scope creep" over the course of the project. Scope creep happens when you propose or promise to deliver a certain defined product or service within fixed parameters. As the project progresses, customers start to add attributes to products or expectations for you providing additional services.

In my world, this often happens with websites. Building a website is easily defined as a certain number of pages, with a predefined set of features. The scope creep comes in when clients expect you to automatically add search engine optimization or analytics and training as part of that package. I have to explain that, no, those are add-on services. They take me additional time and resources and, depending on the client, may or may not be worth my—or the client's—time and expense. The clearer you are about setting and managing client expectations, the better chance you have to underpromise and overdeliver. You want to avoid creating unhappy ex-customers who eat away at your reputation.

Create a value proposition that people can trust

One of the best tools to manage a business, and clients' expectations, is to create a value proposition: define what you do in a way that shows clients the value of your product or service in terms of their expected return on investment (ROI).

As a marketing company, my value proposition is this:

- Marketing should always be an investment and never an expense. If you spend $100, you should make $300: $100 to pay me, $100 for your time and investment, and $100 profit. If we don't expect a three-fold return on your investment, then we should not do the project.

Now, I can't always guarantee a 3 to 1 return on investment, but it sets what I do apart from my competition. I can't help those who don't want to be active and participate in the process. Again, that's not what I offer. I tell customers, "I am in the business of making you more money."

I have had some projects where I could not live up to my 3 to 1 return promise, but many more times I've made clients not just 3 to 1, but sometimes 5 to 1 or 10 to 1, and even (for a lucky few) 25 to 1 or more in profits. You can bet that those folks are my best sales force.

My value proposition also provides a way to quantify whether what I can do for a client will be successful. For instance, a potential client contacted me for help using social networking to promote his book. He asked what that would cost, but before I would give him numbers, I asked what his profit per book was. He told me his publisher would pay him 50¢ per book sold. That means for every $1000 he paid to promote, he would have to sell 2000 books. Based on my 3 to 1 ratio, I would have to help him sell 6000 books for every $1000 he spent. Social marketing can do only so much. The books-sold goal was clearly unattainable and I graciously declined the project. The client not only understood my reasoning but appreciated my honesty.

If you don't believe you can provide value to a potential customer, you need to be honest with yourself AND the prospect. Even if people beg you to help them, you take a huge chance of putting your reputation in jeopardy if you agree knowing you can't reach the target they need.

Testimonials and recommendations are golden

This leads directly to second way to obtain trust, through recommendations, testimonials, and reviews. Nothing is more powerful in driving customers from a Google or LinkedIn search than for searchers to find positive, glowing reviews of your business and your work.

Recommendations can be unsolicited or solicited. Unsolicited recommendations are heart-felt endorsements of satisfaction with your products or services from people impressed enough that they need to say thanks. These can be the most powerful way to build trust because people are writing or speaking (in the case of a voicemail message) from the heart. Solicited recommendations result from people agreeing when you ask them to provide a written, spoken, or video testimonial about you and your business.

LinkedIn is an excellent tool through which to solicit and manage recommendations and testimonials. Although you don't often get to edit or review testimonials and reviews. LinkedIn is one rare exception, allowing you to choose what recommendations you'll show on your profile.

If you need more recommendations, ask for them from connections on LinkedIn with whom you have actually done business. Just be prepared to reciprocate with a positive review for them as well.

I call recommendations outside of social media like LinkedIn testimonials. These normally come in the form of letters and/or emails. Use them to promote your business by simply copying and pasting the text (or retype it) into your testimonials page. Your website does have one, right?

For testimonials, it's good practice to identify the source using the first name and the first letter of the last name (example - a testimonial from me would end with "- Brian B."). If you are going to use someone's full name and/or business, be polite and ask for permission first. Most people are flattered to have their words used "in print."

Another way you can to add testimonials to your website is to gather your recommendations on LinkedIn, then copy and paste them into your testimonials page. Remember, the value from these testimonials comes for their being direct quotes: don't change the wording. You can delete pieces if you want shorter posts, just don't re-write them to make them look better or stronger.

As this book goes to press, LinkedIn has started something call Endorse Me to create more interaction between users. This generic endorsement is not the same as a specific recommendation. I cover this more in the chapter 20.

Don't forget to ask

Positive reviews on Google, Yelp, Merchant Circle, Yahoo Local and other sites can be some of the most convincing factors leading people to trust you enough to pick up the phone and call you, or visit your website and fill out a request form, or send you an email. Think about being on the other end of that transaction. Do you read reviews before purchasing a product or service? Most of us do.

I have been asked more than once about how to deal with a negative review. You can't pick up the phone and dispute a malicious post with Google. Indeed, few websites have any system in place to let you deal with the problem. The only way to meet a bad review head-on is to get tons more positive ones and push the bad-mouthing post further and further down the list of reviews. One bad review with only three good ones can create a reasonable concern for potential customers. One cranky reviewer surrounded by a hundred happy ones will hardly get noticed, or be recognized as an outlier — someone who's never happy.

Recommendations and reviews are your biggest asset in building trust with those who are just getting to know about you, your products and/or services! Always ask satisfied customers for reviews and recommendations, preferably as soon as you complete a sale or project. Manage your reviews, nurture recommenders, and most certainly, be aware of whatever anyone posts about you.

Recognize reputation management as an essential part of your marketing strategy. Whether you like it or not, it's part of the new reality in this 'Google - Search For It' world.

The TRUST phase of KNOW, LIKE, and TRUST is the most transactional part of the equation; it leads most directly to sales. You've reached your end game when those who trust you become the voices for your business. Their voices speak volumes to potential clients. Ultimately, you can't get there without providing excellent products and service, and service over and above customer expectations.

CHAPTER 9: REVERSE NETWORKING

BACON-IZMS

- You've worked hard to build relationships, recycle them

- Communicate new information to existing clients

- Stay in touch with your past

- The past connects the dots to your future

- Old connections can lead to new and better opportunities

You've worked hard to build relationships, recycle them

Some of your most valuable assets are your existing relationships. You have invested much time and money getting people to KNOW, LIKE and TRUST you enough to buy from you and work with you. Too often we tend to laser-focus on generating new business and forget to nurture former or existing relationships.

In a very disposable world, recycling has become über important. Our family puts out three recycle bins each week and only one trash can every other week because we focus on what we can do to make a difference. What if you put more time and effort into recycling relationships rather than only trying harder than ever to get new business?

I grew up on the East Coast... and no trip to the Jersey Shore was complete without a carousal ride. The carousels usually had two or three rows of horses, chariots and special animals like giraffes. You climbed on and got to ride for up to five minutes. That gave almost more excitement than any little kid could handle. When it was our turn, we would run to get one of the outer ponies. That's where you had the chance to grab a brass ring, which gave you a free ride. What does that have to do with business?

Many will tell you that getting new business equals grabbing the brass ring –the ultimate prize. This leads us to run hard to get to the outer ponies—to grab that new business. But you may be better served by some-times running towards your inner circle, the clients or customers you already know.

I spend a lot of time networking. At one point, I was going to 26 meetings a month. I have piles of business cards on my desk, all of which I have scanned into my contact manager and email programs. I work hard to start, build and foster relationships.

But one day I had an epiphany. Although I did commu-nicate with my past customers, I had not wholeheartedly re-invested in them by nurturing those relationships. I realized that I might just be spending too much time trying to get the brass ring of new business and not enough time enjoying the ride—appreciating those I'd already done business with.

New relationships accounted for a large part of my past success but reviewing my financials in Quickbooks showed me that more than half my business now comes from repeat business, or from new relationships associated with past clients.

Stay in touch with your past

As you look forward, it helps to take a look back at what got you to where you are today. Here are some things to think about before you forge into the potential of possibilities.

- Before setting sales projections for next year, next month or next week... review who you worked with last year.

- Re-connect with them and get some feedback. See if they need help or clarification with whatever you did for them.

- Ask them to give you a testimonial.

- Ask them if they think of anyone else in their circle of influence that could benefit from your services!

I am not saying stop trying to grow your business through starting new relationships. I am just asking you to treat those you've already done business with as the valuable resources they should be!

Communicate new information to existing clients

What's new with your business—or theirs—since you last worked for or sold to a former customer? Check these suggestions to get your brain pumping out ideas on news your former contact could use.

- For customers you've trained through classes or webinars, what additional materials or training could you offer that group? Could other past customers benefit from the knowledge and experience you've gained?

- What technology or information are you following, and how can your customers benefit from that? I try to keep up with the (almost daily) changes to Facebook and communicate this news to people that I have worked with through posts and training videos.

- Are you learning from monitoring other clients' data? I have learned so much about trends, SEO and traffic generation from tracking my customers' accounts for them, and those lessons can help others.

- Could you help people better understand trends and avoid pitfalls in your industry? How can you use your data or experience to help others enhance their business in the future?

Always reaching for that brass ring of new or bigger or better business relationships may cause you to forget those who got you started on the ride in the first place.

Stay in touch with your past

This is what I call reverse networking... using traditional and social media to continue relationships with current and past customers who you may not get see face-to-face very often. Even if you generate no new business from them, they already KNOW, LIKE, and TRUST you enough to provide referrals and recommendations. (And don't be shy about asking for these!) Continuing to invest time, energy and resources in past relationships can go a long way to help grow your business in the future.

The past connects the dots to your future

When I walk our dog Buddy Guy, I get a half hour of uninterrupted time to explore new and cool audio books. One I have recently listened to was the biography of Steve Jobs from Apple. He was an interesting dewd, always driven to change the world by doing the unthinkable and impossible. So let the Steve Jobs quotes begin...

"If you haven't found it yet, keep looking. Don't settle. As with all matters of the heart, you'll know when you find it. And, like any great relationship, it just gets better and better as the years roll on"

"You can't just ask customers what they want and then try to give that to them. By the time you get it built, they'll want something new."

"Again, you can't connect the dots looking forward; you can only connect them looking backwards. So you have to trust that the dots will somehow connect

in your future. You have to trust in something – your gut, destiny, life, karma, whatever. This approach has never let me down, and it has made all the difference in my life."

The takeaway here is, you need to keep up with past clients, vendors and other connections.

Old connections can bring new and better opportunities

I have given a lot of presentations to people looking for work. I teach them to use LinkedIn, Twitter and other social media to find work, yes, but more importantly, to get a leg up on the competition.

I have heard, more than once, "I don't want to put on my LinkedIn profile that I worked for 'ABC Company' because I was fired from there and it will look bad on my resume." I did not leave Arthur Anderson in the most graceful way either, but adding that part of my work history to my profile, gave me given the opportunity to connect with more than 168,000 people! Why would I not do that? Since then, I have had more than a few of them reconnect as friends and present opportunities as clients and referral sources.

In the recent down economy, people applied for every job under the sun. Even if they had no experience or qualifications, they would send resume on the chance that they might be seen as a candidate for another position. All this did was pile 600+ resumes on the desk of an already overworked human resources person. This diluted the opportunity for those who had the experience to make them prime candidates for the position.

My neighbor lost a six-figure job. Rather than just follow the lemmings and submit resumes to every job, he found an interesting way to stand out from the crowd.

When he found a job opening with a company he respected, which we'll call ABC Corp, he would search ABC Corp. on LinkedIn, looking for connections who worked there or who knew people working at ABC Corp. Then he posted a LinkedIn message, "Do you know anybody at ABC Corp.? I am applying for a job and would love some help making a connection." He got replies and made the most of the "in" this gave him.

By identifying someone who actually worked in the company that had a job he wanted, he could get that 'friend of a friend' to print out his cover letter and resume, and walk them down to the company's HR office, thus getting his resume on the top of the pile. Did it work, you ask? Better than expected.

While most people felt happy settling for jobs way below their skill level and pay scale, he landed a perfect job with a major corporation at nearly the same level as he'd had in his previous job. This, my friends, is reverse networking at its finest. He used connections in his past to propel his future.

So don't neglect the power of your current or past connections. They can become the most powerful resource in your arsenal. While others may want you to spend all your time, energy and resources on finding that next, bigger new client, customer or job... I encourage you to explore how to capitalize on the connections in your past.

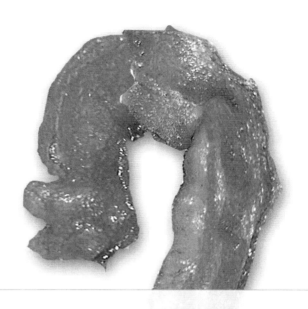

PART 2: BUILD A
WEB FOUNDATION

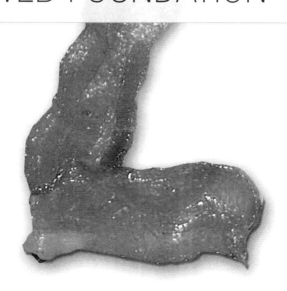

assume you sit in one of two camps:

The NEW GUARD is trying to get a grasp on how to maximize their current presence on the internet.

The OLD GUARD, who grew up in the newspaper, Yellow Pages and postcard world of advertising, is trying to play catch up.

In this second section, members of each camp will find nuggets, but will also have to bear with some "Well, duh" points. You must understand where we have been and where we are now before you can define where we are going.

If I'd written this book only for, say, dog sitters, defining a path to an optimal internet presence would be easier. But I know some of you are financial planners, carpenters, real estate agents, government employees, widget sales people, CEOs or even funeral directors. Each business or person has a unique social DNA.

I hope to explain some of the basics, even some that may be to rudimentary or may be over the top for some of you, but bear with me... it will all make sense sooner than you think!

CHAPTER 10: HAKUNA MATATA & THE CIRCLE OF LIFE

BACON-IZMS

- Your website anchors your social network

- Measure website traffic

- Feed your website more traffic

- Lather, rinse, repeat

- Market hardest when you are busiest

- Plan the work and work the plan

You remember the movie, The Lion King? If you had a kid in the '90s, you probably remember it all too well. This Disney classic includes two very memorable phrases:

- The first phrase, Hakuna Matata, a Swahili phrase, can be translated, "There are no worries."

- The second phrase, the Circle of Life, carries the main theme of the movie.

So I mean this chapter's title to communicate, "You'll have no worries if you understand internet marketing's circle of life."

Your website anchors your social network

It all starts with your website, your networking foundation. When people come to your website, does it make sense? Does the home page/landing page answer these questions in 30 seconds or less?

- What you do?

- What is your brand?

- What are you offering?

- Where do you want them to go next?

Many businesses have a "set it and forget it" attitude about their websites. But, just like plants, websites need tender, loving care and nurturing. Chapter 11 will cover more about website design specifics.

Measure website traffic

Next up on the website life: needs list comes measurement.

- How did people get to your website?

- Where do they go once they get there?

- How long do they spend on your site or each page?

- What page are they leaving from?

All of that data should open your eyes to what's really happening on your website. You need to know how people use it (or don't) to make changes that improve your website's performance.

Feed your website more traffic

The last component the website circle of life needs is food. What is feeding traffic to your website? You can and should use a combination of tools and sources. Everything from face-to-face networking to Facebook, Google to Groupon, post cards to Pinterest and TV to Tweets. Every activity, whether in person, in the media, or online can generate new traffic to your website.

Lather, rinse, repeat

Now that you've identified your circle of (social networking) life, work with it. Use the tools and techniques I'll explain in Chapter 11 to drive traffic to your website. Measure the effectiveness of your website now and analyze the results. Then, update the website, using your newly formed insights to keep what is working and change what is not. And then... lather, rinse, repeat. It's a neverending cycle that leads to growing success when done right.

It may sound like more effort than you want to put in. You may have liked your "set-it and forget it" website approach, but that just will not cut it anymore. If your website never changes, people have little or no reason to return, ever. You need change to continue generating interest. Measure the results with each change and adjust further accordingly.

I have seen it time and time again: People set up a website and wait for SEO to do the work. I have set up dozens of Google Analytics accounts that clients have never logged into or reviewed.

Some people take a stab at setting up Google Adwords accounts. Ok, Adwords can drive people to the home page of your website, but you can't expect that your new prospects have some kind of ESP that tells them what you want them to do next.

Without all three aspects of the Circle of Life working like a fine-tuned engine, our online marketing efforts can sputter and fizzle. How do I know this? First off, I have listened to and learned from some of the best in the industry. I am constantly going to webinars, reading books or listening to audio books and scouring blogs or listening to podcasts. Next, I use myself as the test kitchen. I do trial and error on my own marketing efforts. I find what works and keep tweaking it. Then I apply it to client projects and help them do the same.

I have seen clients go from a few website visits a day to 30-50 a day, leading to measurable increases in new revenue streams (and for me, great sources of referrals).

All operating businesses have time and/or money resources. Some have more of one and less of the other. If you are so busy that you don't have time to market, hire someone to do it. If you are short on funds, then you should spend more time learning how to market and doing it yourself.

Market hardest when you are busiest

One of the most important times to market your business is when you are at your busiest. It's when business goes slack that people tend to panic and try to market harder. Unfortunately, when you are not busy, you may not have the funds to run successful campaigns. Also, you'll see a lag between when you start marketing and when people make buying decisions. It could be mere days, but weeks are more likely... and in some cases, you need years of work and waiting before prospective customers need what you offer. So ask yourself, are you proactive or reactionary with your marketing efforts?

Plan the work and work the plan

Another issue I see is people trying to market without any sort of plan. Making a full marketing plan is a valuable exercise but, just as with business plans, they can be too rigid for today's fluid marketplace. You could plan to get 150 fans on Facebook but then, all of a sudden, Pinterest is generating more traffic to your website than you expected. Should you ignore that and keep working on Facebook? Keeping your marketing relevant means being flexible in response to changes in the marketplace and in communication technology.

I am a big fan of quarterly plans and monthly reviews. I am also a fan of weekly changes. I have a calendar reminder set to update my website every Saturday morning. I am not talking about revamping the whole thing every week, just applying anything that I have learned in the last week.

I have a WordPress database website. So at the very least I update whatever plugins need that. Maybe I add a new plugin I've learned about, or try a new SEO technique I've learned. The point is, I am driven to keep my website as fresh and as leading edge as humanly possible. And that's just my main website. I also run websites for each of my businesses and countless others I manage for clients.

The point being that you make a plan to update, maintain, refresh and grow your website. Review the plan monthly for changes in traffic levels and unforeseen traffic sources and review the plan quarterly to see if it is meeting your goals and helping you generate revenue.

Your social media sites also have metrics.

- How much interaction are you getting in Facebook, LinkedIn and Twitter? Pinterest for business recently added analytics as well.

- Is your email newsletter getting better than 25% opens?

- How many clicks to your website do your outbound emails generate?

- What other sources can you measure and evaluate?

Make the circle of life work for your business. Get your website home in order and keep it up. Measure everything and drive as much traffic back home as you possibly can.

CHAPTER 11:
HOMEWARD BOUND

BACON-IZMS

- Your home should invite people in

- Give the people YOU want what THEY want from your website

- 3 keys: easy to navigate, nice to look at, user-centric

- 5 must-haves: Home, About, Products, Testimonials, Contact

- Ask for (and pay for) help

Your home should be inviting

Home... it's safe, comfortable and where you can be yourself. Dorothy from the Wizard of Oz said there's no place like it, ET wanted to phone to it and cowboys found it on the range. Whether you have a mobile home, apartment, condo, townhouse, single family, or mansion... home is where your heart lives.

When it comes to marketing your business online, your website is your home. People tend to treat their websites like their business lives there. They decorate the site with art to make it feel cool or homey, depending on the business. They often post tons of information,known as brochureware, to make sure the site carries every possible piece of information about the business. They shower the site with pages that link to pages that link to other pages, because they want it to be comprehensive. If your website means to be your business' personal playground, then, fine. Do whatever you want.

Realtors will tell you that, if you want to sell your house faster, you have to paint those walls that you paid thousands faux painting to match your furniture, refinishing them in white or a neutral beige. You have to remove knickknacks, minimize furniture to make rooms look bigger. You have to remove all your signature ceramic chickens and all the mint-green mini appliances from your counters. You have to make your house look as homey as possible, but at the same time like a blank canvas (without making it look abandoned). Only then can people imagine their lives in your house. Those are the attributes your website needs also... It's Not About You!

Think about what would matter if you were a guest in a house.

- Is the kitchen functional and inviting?

- Are the bedrooms comfortable and not cluttered?

- Can you easily find a restroom if you need it?

So how does that translate to my website, you ask?
The kitchen is your **navigation**: is it functional, ergonomic (making the most-used information most accessible).

The bedrooms are the individual **pages**... are they cluttered with information, or are they simple to read with clean graphics?

The bathroom... well, when you gotta go... when you need or want to **contact** someone, is it easy to do?

Seriously, how much do you love having to go find an attendant and ask for a key when you really need to use the facilities. Quite apart from the embarrassment of announcing to the world, or at least everyone in line, that you are going to the bathroom), it takes precious time. Then, once you get there, it's not even clean. Returning the key to the attendant tells a new group of waiting people that you've just relieved yourself. Disturbing, isn't it?

Well, some websites treat their visitors the same way. They conceal their contact information and make you jump through hoops to find it when you have a question or a need.

Why do they do that? Because the company doesn't want to talk to you. It costs money every minute you interact with a paid or contracted employee. Some companies even make you go through voice-prompt hell only to end up talking to someone with a script, someone from India or Columbia or some other place where $1 per hour hires people to field your interruption to the company's money-making machine.

You hate that, don't you? Yet time and again, people clutter their business house (their website) with design, not function, putting their contact information at the bottom of the page in tiny type, or only on the Contact Us page because they've decided it's not visually appealing. This is what happens when people look at their website through their own eyes and not those of site users, their potential customers.

Don't get me wrong, some awesome designers who get this. But a lot of designers transitioning from print to web don't. Print traditionally has a single preferred flow pattern: it starts with a headline, then guides you through the features and benefits and ends with a call to action at the bottom of the page. On websites, the call to action cannot wait that long or appear that far down. You need to gently scatter "what net" suggestions throughout your content. But the details of design choices and content development are topics for an entirely different book. The ultimate question here is, what do you want from your users?

Give the people YOU want what THEY want from your website

I hope I have convinced you to look at your website through your clients' or potential customers' eyes. Now, ask yourself, "What do I want them to do when they get there?" Let me start by saying that no website that is not purely eCommerce has ever made a sale! Let me repeat that... There has never been a site in the history of the world (including those by cavemen painted on cave walls), that has ever made a sale unless it is purely ecommerce! Why? Because only people can make sales.

That means that your primary reason to own a website is to generate a phone call or an email or a contact-form request. Even if you website is purely informational (a blog site, for instance), you are trying to create human interaction through comments (a variant on contact-form requests). Once again, you need to stimulate human interaction.

If you have an eCommerce website or you are doing lead capture for future transactions, that's another thing. You can find some great programs and books (maybe even another one of mine coming soon), to deal with that philosophy and audience. This chapter focuses on those businesses looking for websites to generate phone calls and emails (and ultimately sales).

3 keys: easy to navigate, nice to look at, user-centric

Some people think that just having a good website is the key to online success. But I have to ask, in your opinion, what constitutes a good website? Beauty (or good in this case) is in the eye—and hand and mind—of the beholder. Let's explore those three aspects.

- **For the Hand: make it easy to navigate**. Your website visitors generally have two attributes: good muscle memory and short attention spans. Good muscle memory means that people have a pre-defined expectation about how website navigation should work. They expect pages to be labeled in a way they understand and in a predictable order.

You have two minutes and three clicks to get your main message across. After that you will see a drop off in interaction or even worse, an exit from your website.

I see a common practice with websites I call the Microwave Effect. When microwave ovens first came out, they had all kinds of different user interfaces. Some had buttons, other dials and others had some combination of both. After a while of retail evolution, every microwave has a button called "Popcorn." You push it, it senses the bag of microwave popcorn and cooks it to perfection.

Today, people expect your website to have the web version of the microwave popcorn button. In other words, people (and search engines) expect certain pages to have certain content and in the expected order.

They expect your home page to be called "Home," not "Welcome" or "Yo Dewd!" "About Us" should be about you and your company and usually right next to Home, while your "Contact Us" page is usually the last page listed in the menu.

Use of these pages shows up well on a tool like Google Analytics, but knowing how people want to use their hand to navigate your website is key.

- **For the Eye: nice to look at**. The internet is becoming more and more visual. Ever since Pinterest jumped into the social media mix, Facebook, Twitter and LinkedIn have moved to raise the bar on their visual content and interaction as well. So, if you want to know what the bar is for your website, look at those four websites.

Animated gifs, moving buttons and cartoony stock art shout outdated design now. Contemporary websites feature clean, creative and distinctive photography. Websites have to make the business brand clear through carefully selected colors and fonts that complement the photo visuals.

And the rampant small business trend of just using plain stock photos (like those from IStockPhoto.com) without some added creativity? Nothing screams "stock art" like seeing the exact same graphic on a competitor's website. So many tools let you add personality to your own photos or stock art: use them. Just look at what you can do with free apps like Instagram.

Creative graphics set the tone of a website. They can be illustrations, charts and infographics, or awesome photos. One picture is worth a thousand words, but if the art doesn't support or feels disjointed from your words, they will distract viewers from your message.

Your website header forms the common element throughout the site, appearing on every page. Some types of sites may need different headers for different sections, but you don't want to create a completely different metaphor in each section. Consistency builds continuity. You can change the main graphic and wording, but don't also change position, fonts and colors of everything in each new section.

The same goes for graphics throughout the website. You can change page orientation (landscape vs. portrait), maybe throw in a different theme look and feel for each section, but have some overall consistent plan that makes visual and logical sense to your end users! Try to find a look and feel that enhances your brand, your message and the user experience, without getting in the way of WHY your audience came to the website in the first place.

- **For the Mind: user-centric**. A mind is a terrible thing to waste, and so is your viewers' time. It used to be the norm for every web page to read like a manifesto for your products and services and why your website was the de facto place to be. Then the SEO guys got their hands on your text and pages became so keyword-laden as to be almost unreadable by a casual visitor.

Don't think of your website content as your be-all/end-all opportunity. Think of the website as a tool to create interest. You will get more opportunities to interact and answer questions, especially if the site forms part of an overall marketing campaign. Too often, businesses want their site to be everything to everyone, which dilutes and glazes people's eyes over and confuses them more than helps.

Well-written words create opportunities for more interaction. They can spark a desire to learn more They can lead to more questions to which you respond with useful answers. Good text leads users to ask questions like these:

- Do I know what I want or need?

- Did coming to this website meet my original need? Or better yet, did I learn a new way to understand my needs and wants?

- How can this site's product or service make my business better or more profitable?

Your website's goal should be to create or enhance your business relationship with a potential, new or existing client or customer. In most cases, this ends you want to generate an email or the opportunity for a phone call, from customer to you or you responding to a site-user's query or comment.

In Google's eyes, the optimum website text content is 300 words per page. Using no more than 300 words, you must carefully craft each page for content and readability first, SEO content second.

Write and post as if your business depends on each word. Would that 300 words work as an excellent elevator speech, or are you just BLAH, BLAH, BLAHing users into a coma? Be real and beg you as an awesome first step to creating content that will get your message across AND give users a sense of connection.

And PLEASE, never EVER trade readability for Search Engine Optimization. If you have a reader's eyes on your site, why would you sacrifice that user's experience in mere hopes of luring new readers? That is counter-productive. I have to assume that you worked to get someone to your website, so make it worth their time and your efforts when they arrive! Make your content short and compelling. Have a point (or call to action) in mind.

Showing honest, deliberate intentions will go a long way to building LIKE and TRUST in your audience!

I cannot tell you how many of the phone calls, emails and web inquiries I get from SEO companies who promise to make my website or a client's website number one in Google. I wish I had as many phone calls, emails and web inquiries that ask me, "How can I communicate with my potential customers better?"

SEO is often over-hyped, sold as the Vitamin C that will prevent colds and cancer. In reality, exercise (good content once someone gets to your website) is much more effective than throwing time and/or money at a process you don't fully understand.

I am not anti-SEO. It has its place and value. But I am more pro good user experience. SEO can enhance traffic, but if you are sending people to the 3-day-old fish of websites, you won't get them to eat up what you offer or recommend it to others.

5 essential pages: Home, About, Products/ Services, Testimonials, Contact

Some of the best and most successful websites I have built only have ONE page! A few of them have gotten their owners so much business that those owners have no desire (or reason) to expand them. These sites do not flaunt the typical sales pages, where you scroll and scroll past multiple offers and calls to actions. They are simple, one-page sites that often fit in a single normal browser window.

Don't just treat your websites like a printed brochure. Too often a company's website only covers features and benefits that the business thinks viewers need to know. Remember, viewers want to get to KNOW, LIKE and TRUST you. You help them do that by talking WITH them, not AT them. To do this, you have to give them key answers as quickly and easily as possible:

- Am I in the right place?

- Who is this company?

- What do they do?

- What do others have to say about them?

- How do I get in touch with this business?

So, give them what they want. You can organize the answers on five pages, or on a single page with five sections. Home, About Us, Our Products/Services, Testimonials and Contact Us.

Home: Are you super clear about what you do or sell, or are you trying to make people guess, hoping they dig deeper into your website to find out?

Your home page should be totally clear about what your business does: the value it offers through the solutions it provides. Next, you should provide clear indications of what they should click next for more information. Trying to tell your whole story on the Home Page is a mistake. You have between 10-30 seconds of user attention here. Don't waste it making users scroll or hunt for information, or you will see a high Bounce Rate (people leave your website from that page).

About Us: Here, you give viewers some insight into what experience you have, or what is the history of your company.

What makes you qualified to be a solution of choice? You're building KNOW on this page through background about you or your business. Share your experience, philosophies, or something fun that defines your brand. Showcase your staff, your facilities and other pluses, such as awards or certifications, staff volunteer commitments and community involvement. You may need additional pages to give sufficient space for everything if you also include history, mission and vision statements, news, interviews and anything else you think would help, potential customers feel they KNOW and might LIKE, you.

Products/Services: Give a simple and clear description about what you have to offer the user.

This section works on creating LIKE by explaining what problem(s) your products and/or services solve and why you have the right solution for them. Use additional pages or downloadable PDFs to dig into more details or feature and benefits.

Don't try to over-explain. Make your explanation concise but compelling. Encourage them to dig deeper through the About Us pages, or by a call to action to "Contact Us".

Testimonials: How do past or current clients feel about your offerings?

The more emotional, heartfelt and descriptive your testimonials the better! Length is not as important the emotion expressed by the reviewer. That gratitude or delight forms the lever that moves viewers to want to TRUST. When testimonials come across as real and sincere, they can go a long way to getting people to take the next step... Contact!

Tip: You can find testimonials in a lot of places. The best ones come unsolicited, from places like LinkedIn, emails, letters, even voice mail. Copy online testimonials from places like Facebook or LinkedIn and paste them verbatim (unedited!) on your Testimonial page or section. If they come from less public sources (letters, emails, voicemails), ask the person giving you those good words for a written confirmation that they approve its use on your website. Easiest way to get that? Send them a return letter or email reading as follows:

Dear [satisfied customer name]:

Thank you for letting me know how much our work meant to you. We would like to feature this endorsement on the company website: [include the quote you plan to use]. Please let us know if this is OK with you and whether we can use your full name or whether you prefer to be identified by first name and last initial.

Contact Us: Often treated as a throwaway extra, this page is the whole point of your website: getting potential customers to contact you.

Unless you run an ecommerce website, your goal should always include encouraging users to contact you. You want to hear their needs or wants, so you get the chance to communicate directly with them, answering their questions in a way no website can.

So, first of all, this means your contact information shouldn't just hide on the contact page. Users don't want a scavenger hunt. At a minimum, your company's email and phone/fax should appear on the header and/or the sidebar of every page. If the physical location of your business matters, include your street address too. The easier you make it for people to reach you... the more often they just may do that!

I am not dismissing your need for a well-designed or efficiently programmed website. I'm simply explaining that getting users to do what YOU expect depends on you giving them what THEY expect.

Ask for (and pay for) help

For your business website, what matters is how your visitors and end users perceive it. Very few of us are blessed with skills in user interface design, graphic art creation or Photoshop, and creative writing talent plus SEO knowledge. If you excel at one of these skills, you're steps ahead of many businesspeople. If you're good at two of them, you are exceptional. If you have all three, you can put this book down. You don't need it; you need a good financial advisor to help you handle all the money you're making!

In reality, you possess enough skills to start the web design process, but you will do yourself and your business an injustice unless you find good power partners in the areas where you DO NOT excel, whether that be technical website design and management, graphic design and branding, or writing and content management.

Without trying to be to disrespectful, I have to say I know companies that spend more money on giveaway pens than on a killer logo. Some spend more money on Starbucks in a month than they spend on their website in a year. And hire a writer? Perish the thought!

People will search for offers of free or $99 logos. The people providing these have no interest in you or your business other than hoping your $99 credit card payment clears.

What can your clients find for $99 versus $500? Or $9 versus $50? Does a low-ball price get them good value, fully enhancing them, their company, or their brand?

I'm sure you charge a higher price for your products or services because of your customer service, experience or return on investment. So why would you expect to get high quality design work for bargain-basement prices?

I know my strengths (and I give good value with many of them) and I know my weaknesses (and I am humbled at MOST of them). I tell clients when I first meet them, "You do NOT want me writing your content." My wife proofreads all my blogs because I just cannot see mistakes. This book exists because of a cooperative effort with people who ARE writers and proofreaders. (Without them, I guarantee you would not have made it this far!)

I am not asking you to spend money you don't have, just to realize the difference between being frugal and passing up a valuable investment. I am sure you have people in your network who can either help you, or point you to people who can help you. Make an investment in your business and relationships that can help propel you and your business to the next level.

Maximize your strengths, use your experience and know when to ask for help so your website succeeds by making users' hands, eyes and minds happy!

CHAPTER 12:
MEASURE THIS

BACON-IZMS

- Web stats rarely tell you the whole story

- Analytic tools provide you with useable data.

- Remember: 2-3 clicks and 2 minutes

- Small business websites average 20-30 visitors/day

- Use measurement to plan website changes/updates

In the last chapter, we explored the purpose of having a good website, one that serves your customer base or target audience well. Next, you need to get some sense of the traffic going to your website.

I have heard people say their website is getting 250,000 hits per month. Although that may be true based on the reports they are getting, it's not an accurate count of how many PEOPLE are getting to the website, or of how they are using it.

The many ways to measure website traffic include both free and paid services. Whichever too(s) you choose, you must use something to benchmark your traffic and let you track how actions you take affect it. You can bench-mark yourself against your own numbers, but I prefer to use a tool that lets me benchmark my web traffic against other websites, both within and outside of my industry.

Some people rely on the built-in tools offered by their webserver. These tools use the server logs to measure things like hits and pages viewed. The problem with most of these is they give you a skewed reality of what is really happening with traffic to your website.

These report the data being served up by your website. A hit can be anything from a graphic to link or text being sent to the internet. A single, very complex webpage can generate up to 1000 hits from a single viewer, depending on how it was built and how the server's tool parses the log data. How? A page can create hits to all the pages it links to, so one page can generate 5-25 page "views" whether or not the user follows those links, depending on how your server log interprets these hits. By this logic, the 250,000 hits your server's tool report may equate to only 250 views of individual web pages. Because the average view will click on 2-3 more links or pages, that means you probably had closer to 60-80 separate people show up on your website. I know, 250,000 sounds so much better, but do you want to plan around a skewed reality or a true reflection?

I am a fan of Google Analytics. You can learn more about that service at www.google.com/analytics. Many more free or paid-for services (Clicky, Kissmetrics and WebTrends, just to name here) give you data as good as if not better than Google Analytics. To review options, just Google 'Google analytics alternatives."

Google gives Google Analytics out for free to any user. Why? Because most people allow Google to share their data, giving Google access to valuable information for use in tracking web activity in general and to interpolate for the sale of Google Adwords. Adwords is how Google makes most of its money (See Chapter 13).

For a free tool, Google Analytics wields incredible power and a wealth of information. You can look at the basics: how many people visited my site this day, week or month and which pages they visited most. But it also allows you to dig way deeper than that. For example, you can see which pages are most likely to be visited after the first page and in what order. You can see which country, state or even town generates the most traffic to a page. You can see which page most people are leaving your website from. You can see what people searched for to find your website and which of your social media drives the most traffic. It even gives you real-time data about who's on your site right now.

This pretty awesome tool is relatively simple to install and use. Simply go to www.google.com/analytics and create an account. If you already have a GMail account, you simply sign up. With most static html websites, you add a small javascript code to allow Google Analytics to track usage. You copy the code from Google and paste it into each webpage you want to track. If your website was made in Wordpress or Drupal, it's even easier: just copy and paste the UA code (the number Google assigns your web property) and paste it into a plugin. That's it! Now you are tracking data from every page in your site.

Once you have a measurement tool installed, give it a few days to collect some data and you can be on your way to better understanding how your website is being viewed and used.

I have set up and now manage more than 100 Google Analytics accounts, so I can share with you a sampling of what I have learned from small, local and large, national businesses alike.

How big your website is or needs to be depends on your business and what your audience needs or expects. I have seen one-page websites for small local businesses that generate more business than an owner can handle. But companies that handle dozens (or hundreds) of products need many more pages to serve their customers, distributors, resellers and sales reps by offering the sales sheets, installation instructions, user manuals and other essential product information online.

Remember: 2-3 clicks and 2 minutes

The average website interaction (your "web visitor") will make 3 clicks and give your site 2 minutes of attention. The 100-500 page website may get 4 or 5 clicks and up to 4 minutes per visit, but not much more. That's the attention span of the average web user. Now you know why Google likes pages that limit themselves to 300 words of copy, since most people don't spend enough time on a page to read more than that.

This short window of opportunity and limited number of pages viewed explains why measurement ranks so important in your overall web strategy. To catch their attention, you need to know:

- Where do people enter your website?

- Where are they coming from?

- Where do they go next?

- What page are they leaving on?

If you have a plan for how you want visitors to move through your website, you can measure whether users in fact follow it.

A good home page will inform the user about what you do. It almost moves their hands for them, to click on a link or button that gets them to the information, product or service they came to your website looking for. That next page should tell them about that product or service in clear, concise language and either direct them to a testimonials page or give a call to action like "Learn More" or "Contact Us" or "Buy Now." (I will save the killer ecommerce website philosophy for another book.) If you do not work to direct page-to-page traffic in light of that 2-3 click/2 minute rule, your website probably won't work like you want it to.

I mentioned earlier that websites don't make sales. People do. More often than not, you should expect to make or receive a phone call or send an email before you close on a deal or a sale. Some people may never get past your home page, because they pick up the phone and call you. Others may want to email you with questions, while others have no problem filling out your form on the contact us page or subscribing to your email newsletter. It's your job to make contacting you as easy as possible.

Of course, Google Analytics cannot measure what happens if web visitors do pick up the phone, or after they email you or fill out a contact form. It's up to you to measure what happens from there. Gather as much data about who came from what source as possible without being overbearing or intrusive. You should have a system in place that measures leads, conversions, referrals and sales. If you don't, consult one of the many good books on that subject.

Small business websites average 10-30 visitors/day

You might also want to know how much traffic your website gets per day or per month. What you should expect or aim for really depends on your business, what it sells, who it sells to and whether you are a local, regional, national or international business.

Consider these baselines for monthly usage, which is a more reliable indicator than daily traffic. Dividing that by 30 (for the roughly 30 days per month), you get your average hits per day. Most local, small service-business sites will get 300-600 hits a month, or an average range of 10-20 per day. Most regional business websites get around 1200-1500 per month (40-50/day). And national sites range around 3000-6000/month or 100-200/day). If your market is very limited, you may get far less traffic. If you audience covers a wide age and demographic range, your site may blow these numbers out of the water. So keep these numbers in perspective from what you know about YOUR business.

You should also look at which days bring more hits than others. If you focus on attracting businesspeople, you will see most of your hits come in during the work week. If your business is consumer-focused, you may see peak visit numbers between Friday afternoon and Sunday night.

Another thing you can measure is bounce rate, the measure of users who get to your website but leave after the first page. The average business has around a 33% bounce rate: 33% of the users who visit your site leave from the page they first visit.

Bots and spiders cause a lot of bounce hits. Search engines and other directories send out bots and spiders to sample your webpage, crawling around to discover what the site is about, or if it even exists. They come to the page, scan it and leave, with a time-on-page equal to 0 seconds. That's the signature of a spider or bot. It's a good thing, because it means your website is being found and made relevant by Google and other search engines.

In some cases, a bounce rate of more than 40% is bad, showing that too many people become disinterested in your website on the first page. In other cases (like my main website), it's not as problematic. I have a bounce rate of 60-70%. I don't worry about that because the majority of people coming to my website coming to read my blog. I expect them to read that one page and leave. Of course, I do hope that a few will read other blog posts, or explore my services pages. I direct them to do that with links in my blog posts and the 30-40% who DON'T leave after one page show I get modest success with this.

Use of a blog will be covered more in the next chapter and in Chapter 26.

Use measurement to plan website changes/updates

The last suggestion in this chapter is **ready-fire-aim**. **Ready** means you are all set; you have your website and your measurement tool of choice. With luck, you also have some idea what you need to measure (new versus returning visitors, or hits increasing or decreasing from a particular activity, for instance). **Fire** happens when you execute your activity (an email, broadcast or podcast, a blog post, a social media interaction, or even a face-to-face networking event). **Aim** involves analyzing the results of the aforementioned **Fire** event to determine its value. If it significantly increased activity, do it again and see if you get similar results. If you see minimal or negative results, you should question whether to continue this approach; it may not suit your business or your audience.

Metrics should be applied to every business activity, but especially every web activity. Sometimes you can wait through three to seven iterations of an email broadcast or social media post before you see some traction start to develop.

Also, don't assume every success will be equally measurable. I have had a few posts in social media that caught lightning in a bottle, getting shared dozens, even hundreds, of times and bringing in dozens or hundreds of comments and likes. Others, which I thought just as potent, fell flat. Stay aware and remain patient as you Ready, Fire, Aim, over and over again!

I have barely scratched the surface of what measuring web traffic can do for you and your business. I hope I've inspired you to check your analytics at least weekly. If you do, you can spot trends and separate those events that help create more traffic from those that just waste time. I check mine almost daily, because I track dozens of daily activities I do on four websites and countless social media pages. I need to check often to know which interactions are bearing fruit and which are just dead branches.

CHAPTER 13:
DRIVE IT HOME

BACON-IZMS

- Update: give people reasons to revisit your website

- Fish for clients: Drive people to your website

- Media or ME-dia

- Traditional media means print, radio, TV

- New Media include Websites, Email, Banner Ads

- Social media harness relationships

In the previous two chapters, we've looked at why a good website forms the cornerstone for most business and you need to measure your site's traffic if you hope to harness the power and capabilities of your website. In this chapter, we take a closer look at the final player in the online trifecta, the traffic itself.

Heavy traffic associated with an urban or suburban commute has a very negative connotation. It causes delays, backups and frustration. But you celebrate heavy traffic on your website as it brings hope for new business. It means that you have attracted the web's attention and that you can look forward with confidence to many potential checking out your business.

The three major concerns with website traffic mirror the measurement mantra of ready, fire, aim:

- Generate the traffic.

- Measure the results.

- Modify your website!

About now, you may hope I will teach you all the secrets to generating mind-blowing traffic for your website, but that's not the most important lesson to learn here. Before you get to mind-blowing levels of traffic, you need to understand what's working and use that knowledge to create the experience users want and expect when they get to your website. If I knew a magic formula for that, this would have been a much shorter book. I would have shared the secret in Chapter 1 and I'd be stashing away my spare money in the bank that I'd own on my private island in the Caribbean.

Update: give people reasons to revisit your website

Modifying your website is a neverending challenge but you must keep up. Nothing tells visitors you don't care like seeing ©1999 at the bottom of your page. Some people are blown away when I tell them that the average life expectancy of a website is the same as or less than that of their last computer.

Most people change their computers every 3-5 years, although this book is being written on a Mac Pro that is 7+ years old. Well, five years ago, the cost of a high-quality, enterprise-type website averaged $3000 to

$5000 so most people expected many years of return on their investments.

Things have changed. The issue for website quality is no longer cost but whether you're creating something dynamic and relevant. A good, responsive website requires more than a set-it-and-forget-it mentality. It requires constant attention, upkeep and TLC (total loving care).

Some people treat their website as a brochure for viewers to read and get sold enough to ask for more information. Others treat their site like the Yellow Pages: just an ad to pull in prospects for the salespeople to talk to. Some make their sites work like a car salesman who yells at people, hoping to beat them into submission. I am here to tell you the magic website is none of the above and yet has aspects of all of the above at the same time.

Fish for clients: Drive people to your website

Measurement lets you see how people find you and what do they do once they get to your website. Your job is to give them what they want while guiding them to what you want: a phone call, an email or some other contact and eventually, a sale.

How you do this is what your measurement data should tell you. The biggest mistake you can make is not using this data to guide the updates in your web content.

How I update my website content is subjective and ever-changing, based on what I have learned from reviewing my site-use data and from other stories, blogs and clients that week. The important point is that I update it at least every week, sometimes every day!

In a world with hundreds of thousands, even millions of Tweets, Facebook posts and LinkedIn updates a day, can you fool yourself that a website last updated weeks, months, or even three years ago could still be relevant? You may not realize that things have changed much but they have. Don't broadcast your ignorance of the need for change to the world, because your competition is probably on top of it.

When I was a little kid, I loved to go down to the local lake and fish. Never for fish to eat, just to catch and release. I used a simple fishing pole with a simple hook. I would put wet bread on the hook and toss it into the water. I was lucky enough to catch and release the occasional bluegill and that's all I wanted to do. When I got older, I became friends with people who took fishing a lot more seriously than I did. They had world-class bass boats, depth finders, multiple reels, many different poles and lines and fancy tackle. They have also learned at what places each type of fish can be found at all times of day and on which lures they'll strike.

Think of trying to find new clients like fishing. You can just cast your net where you are, or you can pay big dollars on software and programs and SEO and so on. But a little knowledge about the fish you are trying to catch can make your job much easier and more effective.

Driving traffic to your website has three components... kind of like fishing has the hook, line and sinker. The sinker is the part of your message that gives it depth, that gets it to the audience you are trying to reach. The line is whatever guides users to your website. The hook is what you use to reel them in.

Too many people treat marketing, and especially online marketing, like fishing with nets, using Yellow Pages and other old-school broadcast marketing techniques. Cast your marketing net out into the water in the right location, and you will get fish. Some you want and some you don't. But with thousands of messages barraging us every day, the net is showing its age. More of the fish you want to haul in are escaping and more of the ones you don't need are eating up precious time that could be spent elsewhere! So how does the sinker, hook, line approach work?

The Sinker: is the client attraction process starts with your planning and placement: social media, advertising and any other activities that add depth to your core business message. Fishermen know that certain fish like to feed at certain depths. Too much weight and your hook sinks too close to the bottom. Not enough weight and it floats near the surface. Having the right sinker weight for your web promotion could mean choosing the right social media, for instance. You want to be promoting someplace that lets your messages hang around where the "fish" feed, dangling on pages your preferred customers visit.

The Hook: Message and media get new prospects to take the hook so you can reel them in for a sale. First, your hook needs good bait, which is the job of your ads and social media. Is your content fresh and attractive and tasty? Your headlines and content should be designed to attract the kind of customers you want. You have to know what fish you are fishing for to figure out what bait these fish like at the depth where your hook lies. This means you need to know your media as well as your preferred customer. An appropriate Facebook or Twitter post might be too frivolous or personal for the audience you reach on a more profession-oriented site like LinkedIn.

So what's your hook? How can you use networking, social media and advertising to drive people to your website? Your goal is to give good (or great), compelling information that intrigues people to click your link(s). What is the message that gets them emotionally charged or wanting to learn more? That is your hook.

If you don't take your choice of hook and bait seriously, you may get a lot of useless but time-consuming nibbles (what car salespeople call tire kickers!). How much time are you wasting trying to convince people that your product or service is the right answer for their needs when your baited hook should not have attracted them?

The Line: Once you get them hooked, can you reel your new prospects in enough to give you their contact information or entice them to contact you? You use motive and measurement to reel new visitors in. Once they have grabbed the bait, you have to lead them where you want them to go.

One of the biggest mistakes online marketers make is driving people to a home page and then letting the visitors choose for themselves which page to visit next. That's like letting a fish choose which net or boat to jump into, it's just as likely to choose open ocean. You want your line to get your prospective customers to the message they expect. This could include a landing page targeted for a specific ad or post. It could also be a specific page already within your website. Don't make visitors decide for themselves where to go next; direct them with your call to action – Buy Now or Contact Us.

It takes the right lure for the right fish. It takes the right bait to get them to bite. It takes a strong enough line to reel them in. You have to know and use the right combination to get the best results. Knowing who you are marketing to and what makes them react, is how you attract people who WANT to interact with you, to KNOW, LIKE and TRUST your products, service and business.

I know I am NO Babe Winkelman (Fish Master Extraordinaire), but still, having the right information and the right equipment can make all the difference! Casting a net reaps quantity, but having a plan, purpose and perseverance can reap the quality you need!

You do promotion yourself. You pay for advertising.

Promotion you do yourself. It could be face-to-face networking where you get out and meet people. It could be presentations that you give to networking groups, business groups, chambers of commerce or any gathering where you can provide educational material about your business or industry. You could teach classes at community colleges or universities.

You can become an information resource, someone who gives interviews for print news sources, online articles or blogs. You can be a guest on a radio show or podcast. Your own blog(s) can be excellent means of promotion, as I will discuss in Chapter 26. You can be a resource on social media by answering questions on LinkedIn, Twitter or Facebook. You can create or participate in webinars. There are hundreds of ways that you can self-promote.

Find opportunities to promote your business through great resources like Help A Reporter Out (HARO) or Bill and Steve Harrison's Reporter Connection. (Google HARO or Reporter Connection to find them on the web.) If you register on these sites, they will send you daily emails detailing opportunities to connect with reporters, bloggers, podcasters, radio and TV shows and more. They handle requests for just about every imaginable industry. Don't expect these to propel you to stardom, but ANY promotion is better than promotion.

Also, some of the outlets that show up in these emails will charge you a fee to participate in their podcasts or presentations. That is not promotion, that is advertising.

Advertising is promotion that you pay for. But sometimes you do need to open up your wallet or checkbook to enhance your brand.

Advertising comes in many forms. I like to break them down into three media segments:

- Traditional

- New

- Social

Yes, sometimes advertising in social media does make sense! More on that later.

Just like promotion, advertising can happen online or offline. Your goal should be to place ads where you can measure results. Websites provide an excellent home base from which to measure the effectiveness of any advertising campaign. Large businesses and corporations can easily justify spending money to enhance a brand. My guess is that, for those of you reading this book, your main concerns involve revenue and sales.

Advertising can do a good job of generating leads as long as you use the right medium to reach the desired audience. You also want measurable (and repeatable) results. Not all people surf the internet looking for you, but ads may prompt into researching you, your brand and your products or services online. So don't discount all old-school techniques, especially if your audience remembers the world before the internet.

Media or ME-dia?

You already know the big difference between "media" and "ME-dia" even if you've never thought about it in those terms. Media are the tools and components of your advertising and communications. They can also serve as the delivery tools that you use, whether print or digital or other.

ME-dia are any communications that constantly focus on the communicator. If you want to create disinterest really fast, just constantly talk about yourself all the time.

Traditional media means print, radio, TV

I consider as traditional media advertising all the things business did before the internet revolution. Many businesses still use these successfully today! You may want to look at flyers, postcards, letters, or other mailer formats that include a link to a special landing page with an offer or coupon. Those do tend to show a higher rate of return for repeat business than with new business.

The phone book is not dead either, although it is on life support. It still pulls in around 15% of search traffic versus people going online and Googling for what you offer. If your audience is senior citizens, a Yellow Page listing may make sense. If you are selling pizzas to 20-somethings, Fuggeddaboudit!

Some businesses still rely on roadside billboards. You can also use the high-tech mini-billboard programs placed in bars, transportation and other high traffic areas. These glorified HD TVs rotate through a set of ads. Even some roadside billboards have gone high tech, with 10-second alternating ads. It's more cost-effective than selling the same number of printed billboard ads, ads that had to be installed and removed manually. And frankly, the digital billboards present more brilliant and interesting displays because they do change frequently.

Don't discount radio or TV advertising. Although they tend to be expensive, depending on what you are selling, they can still be an effective tool. More and more TV commercials are using Twitter handles that then drive traffic to a website. Then you may hear radio commercials that encourage listeners to "Find Us on Facebook".

New media include websites, email, banner ads

I call any one-directional, internet- or data-based electronic media new media. This includes email marketing, text-message marketing, banner ads, adwords and any other internet-based advertise service involving paying to get information about your business on the internet or smart phones.

Of course people want to use free listings like Google maps or places and directories like Yelp, Merchant Circle and Angie's List free. They can help you a lot, especially if you get great reviews from customers, but they're not usually the first place people look on the web. To get to that first place and generate more traffic, you may have to open up your wallet and pay. Google did not get to be a $600/share business by giving everything away, after all.

Social media harness relationships

So if social media and social networking are not advertising then what are they? First and most importantly, they are about building and growing relationships. So that's where the work begins. Who do you want to have a relationship with and where can you meet them? And why (and where) would you pay for greater exposure?

Paid social media comes in a couple of forms. You can buy ads on Facebook, LinkedIn, Twitter and so on. Or you can pay someone to do the posting on your social media pages.

A word about advertising on Facebook in particular: People who click on an ad in Facebook generally want to stay on Facebook. So, if you are going to advertise there, make sure you drive them to your Facebook page or landing pages. Success significantly drops off when you drive them to another website. Facebook advertising works great if you want more fans or to show people your Facebook information.

The second form of paid social media, paying someone to post and interact as you, can work for some businesses. It can also backfire if people get wind that it's just posting for the sake of posting and not relationship building. If the person or company doing the posting for you is well trained and knowledgeable in your industry and brand and can and does answer questions on your behalf, it can work well. If they just ignore or (even worse) misinform, it can have disastrous results.

Ultimately, the best social media interactions happen between two people who know each other. So my advice to you is, be as engaged as possible. If you have an employee, freelancer or third-party company posting on your behalf, check in often and monitor conversations.

No matter what you use to drive more traffic to your website, don't ignore or discount what you learned in Chapters 11 and 12. You have to have a solid, user-friendly and user-centric website that generates phone calls, emails or sales. You have to measure what is working and create and use a Ready, Fire, Aim approach to generating more traffic.

Promotions and advertising are the tools that allow you to generate interest. Social media and social networking are the tools that allow you to build relationships and continue to stay top of mind.

PART 3: DEFINE YOUR AUDIENCE

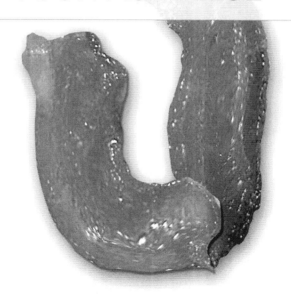

The difference between inbound and outbound marketing in a nutshell:

- Outbound marketing casts a net and hopes you catch enough attention to make it worth the time and efforts.

- Inbound marketing encourages people to search you out and interact with you.

Both traditional and new-media marketing and advertising tend to function as outbound marketing tools. Inbound marketing works primarily through online advertising and social media.

For inbound marketing to work, you have to know two key components:

1. Who is your potential customer or audience?

2. Where are they most likely to see and interact with your messages?

One of the most common mistakes with inbound marketing is treating it like traditional advertising, running with a very general message and hoping it covers all their audiences.

In this section, we will explore how to segment contact programs with plans for each of the groups you want to reach and how your brand plays into your social media marketing plans.

CHAPTER 14: WHAT'S YOUR BRAND?

BACON-IZMS

- A brand defines your product/service/business

- Truth #1 Social media is NOT about advertising!

- Truth #2 BUSINESSES don't buy products or services, PEOPLE do!

- Your online brand is Not About You!

- Your business has its own brand

- Your personal brand is part of your business

- Social networking can build personal and business brands

A brand defines your product/ service/business

Branding means a lot of things to a lot of people. Those who read a lot (or watch) of Westerns may remember the hot iron logo that ranchers apply to the back ends of their cattle, so everyone can identify whose cattle are whose.

A "type of product manufactured by a company under a particular name" (Google's definition) constitutes part of the business application of the branding concept—to provide instant identification for your product, service or company. But, in the real world, brands involve much more than just a product line. A business brand can include a name, logo, slogan and/or the design (colors, fonts and more) associated with a product, service or company. Personal branding, a newer concept, can help garner attention for celebrities... or job seekers.

In one of my favorite 'Old School' books, Tom Peters' *In Search of Excellence*, he explores the Disney Theme Park experience as a brand.

At a Disney property, everyone you meet, from the person who sells you tickets, to the person sweeping up trash, is 'in character'. That character is there to create the perception of a fun experience... for everyone from newborns to grandmas. Employees get extensive training to make sure that YOUR experience the same kind of service and environment whether you visit Disney theme parks in Florida, California, Europe or Far East, or go on a Disney Cruise.

Seth Godin takes that branding concept a bit further. He says in his blog (sethgodin.typepad.com/seths_blog/2009/12/define-brand.html):

Here's my definition: A brand is the set of expectations, memories, stories and relationships that, taken together, account for a consumer's decision to choose one product or service over another. If the consumer (whether it's a business, a buyer, a voter or a donor) doesn't pay a premium, make a selection or spread the word, then no brand value exists for that consumer.

Brands totally transcend our traditional concept of Kleenex = tissue or Coke = soda. They encompass everything from your website, your receipts and your invoices, to the way you communicate with customers, contractors, vendors and others. Your brand includes everything in and around your business.

Some solopreneurs spend hundreds or thousands a month to rent space so their companies look and act bigger than they are (yet). Other people completely wrap their cars or trucks in graphics so they become mobile billboards. I see people showing up at informal networking events in a suit and tie when their actual work requires them to crawl around on the ground. Depending on your budget, brand and business, these approaches can be awesome, or awful!

Some solopreneurs set up do-it-yourself websites that leave you wanting a secret decoder ring to find how you contact them. Others simply cannot communicate in one-on-one situations, either selling too hard or just misunderstanding a potential client's actual needs.

Some of these same people pass out business cards from Vista Print or some other free service, cards using logos bought for $99 or less. Cheap design and printing companies work by shipping projects overseas. This means the people actually working on your logo or card design have no clue what your business does or what your clients expects from a product or service. Is that what you want?

Your brand is the essence of your business and everything you do, especially what you communicate and how you communicate it! I totally understand that you may not have the time or budget to have everything professionally created or executed, but you need to review what you have periodically and ask yourself, "Is this helping or hurting my business?"

Ask your colleagues, clients, vendors, friends and neighbors for some feedback. Think about what they tell you; keep and act on what you find helpful. Toss or file the rest. Let the world be your focus group (unless you can also pay to have people put behind a two-way mirror!).

Truth #1 Social media is NOT about advertising!

I recently met with a client who sells and leases commercial real estate. He asked, "How can I use social media to promote my business?"

I told him, "You don't use social media to promote your business... you use it to promote you!" He looked puzzled so I continued. "Your social media brand may not be exactly what your traditional business brand is, because it has to be entertaining, informative and engaging."

Unfortunately, a whole bunch of businesses don't realize that. They see invoices, purchase orders, sales graphs. They all fall for the Get Rich Quick fallacies out there:

"There's 1 Billion Potential Sales on Facebook"
"LinkedIn Your Sales Machine"
"Tweet for Cash"

But the folk you run across who often annoy you even more are people who have attended webinars and seminars on The Use of Social Media. These sessions have convinced them that they can use social media as a fast and free advertising option. This could not be more further from reality (and success).

Seth Godin has written (sethgodin.typepad.com/seths_blog/2008/12/brands-social-c.html),

---

"Traditional advertising is inherently selfish. It interrupts in order to generate money (part of which pays for more interruptions). That approach doesn't work at a cocktail party, or at a funeral or in a social network"

Truth #2 BUSINESSES Don't Buy Products or Services, PEOPLE DO!

Social media are all about people and their connections. They're about building, growing, fostering, developing and engaging in networks of RELATIONSHIPS. Think about it: What annoys you most in Facebook, LinkedIn or Twitter? Sponsored ads? Or the person who does nothing but sell-sell-sell: self, products and/or services? Facebook is about family and friends first, but you can also use it to connect with clients, vendors and prospects.

How do you measure success and failure in social media? Some would say sales, but I say INTERACTIONS. Look at the posts that have the most likes, comments, shares and re-tweets. They all have one thing in common... ENGAGEMENT, whether sparked by a wedding picture celebrating an anniversary, a joke, or even a political or religious article (although the last one I don't recommend). People who connect with you emotionally will invest their time in your post through liking, commenting on or sharing it.

Author Chris Brogan writes,

"Ask yourself this: in trying to reach others for whatever your goal may be, is it facts or emotions that will win them over? Which do you think plays the bigger role?"

Truth #3 Your online brand is Not About You!

The sheer volume of messages they receive overwhelms people. At best, 25% of your audience opens your emails. Text messages eat up space on our phones. Google ads or snail mail post cards get considered successful with as little as 1-2% click-through or redemption rates. People don't log into their social media to be sold... They log into Facebook to be entertained, check Twitter for news or direct conversations and review LinkedIn to be informed, educated and connected.

Your audience wants you to be YOU, not a salesperson. Laugh, cry, learn, grow... with them. Educate, inform, entertain, engage and commiserate... with them. Do all these things with a sense of creating value. Value your friends' and fans' time, opinions, successes and challenges, and value the ability to grow your relationships. But for the love of all things good and worthy... DON'T SELL AT THEM!

Author John Morgan says,

"You should never take your audience for granted. The attention they give you is a gift. Be alert when you're using social media. Everything you do either works for your brand or against it."

Your business has its own brand

Everything said in this chapter applies to both your business and your personal brand and posts. Just because you also have (and use) a personal profile on any social networking site does not mean that you can ignore any of this advice when posting to your business page. But let's look at the business perspective for a moment.

Your business has probably found a niche or a vertical market (maybe more than one) in which you, your business and your message resonate. Mine has been animals.

My dog Buddy Guy does not have his own website, Twitter account, or Facebook group, but when I post a picture of him, I get an immediate connection with other people who have or love pets. People walk up to me and ask me about him. I even have some friends that bring him treats who have never met him. It's a connection that endures!

We have adopted our last six pets through rescue groups. From that connection have grown opportunities to work with pooper scoopers, groomers, mobile groomers, pet sitters and doggie day care providers. Along the way, I donated a website worth (at the time) $10,000 to a totally volunteer local animal rescue. The group was not only grateful, but totally blown away by that gift.

One job or speaking engagement leads to another. I was offered the opportunity to be a paid keynote speaker at a national A.P.A.W.S (www.apaws.org) convention in San Diego, California. That led to still more pet-related clients. I've continued to get work where I've had the opportunity to give over and above amounts of support to these clients and groups, which I'm happy to do because of my wife's and my passion for animals. From a simple networking meeting, I have grown a niche business within the full spectrum of my business, one that continues to give me referrals, presentation opportunities and credibility in a very tightly knit market segment.

Have you noticed any trends or niche markets that your business has started to serve? If you are a realtor, maybe it's short sales. Maybe golfers, if you are a personal trainer. Maybe neighborhoods with definable income levels for a remodeler, carpet installer, handyman or other tradesperson. And by the way, remember that your current clients talk about you more than you think.

So, how do you go about connecting with these niche or vertical markets online? By posting fun pictures, amusing text, or interesting articles—anything important to you—on Facebook, LinkedIn, Twitter, Pinterest or in a blog or website. This kind of post opens the door for conversations, interactions, comments and relation-ships. If you only post about your products, your services offered or your company all the time, that tells people you care more about their money than them!

Your personal brand is part of your business

Have you ever Googled yourself? What comes up first?

If you use social media tools like LinkedIn, Twitter, Google Plus to their full potential, then your profile page on one of those will come up first. (If you have a fairly common or famous name this becomes a bit more of a challenge. Luckily, most of us don't.)

Your LinkedIn listing often comes up number one because of the amount of traffic LinkedIn gets. Traffic is what makes the right social media so important in promoting your personal brand. Authors know this, because you can have the best book in the world and a slick website to promote it, but you need to list on Amazon.com before your name or book title will rise to the top of a Google search. Once you've associated with a website that has millions of visits a day, many more people can find your name (and, for Amazon, book title) on it.

I give presentations to many diverse groups. For some reason, I get numerous requests from local Rotary Clubs, some of the most friendly, giving, fun people I have ever met. They are hungry to learn about the hot topic of social media, but I had to learn how I should communicate my knowledge to them. I quickly realized that these mostly retired 50- to 80–year old people were incredibly relational, with lifelong friendships and a desire to make their community better, but the newfangled social media tools just did not make sense to them. It's not that they didn't understand the principles. But not only did the technology baffle some of them, the why of social media's importance escaped them. They want to do coffee or call you, not tweet or text you!

The internet has changed everything. I love and respect those Rotarians who already have the right principles and expectations... but the technology is the NEW methodology. People Google everything and read the online testimonials and reviews to determine their best choices. They value their friends' opinions more than strangers'.

Social media starts with SOCIAL for a reason. They're about relationships. Creating online connections takes some risk and effort. That means you have to share and connect with people all around you. You and your likes, hobbies, talents and passions—not your products or services—are why people want to connect with you. What's important to you? If you volunteer, have pets, restore antiques, play sports, eat bacon... people can relate with that!

Social networking can build personal AND business brands

I often hear people say "I just want to post as my business. I don't want to post anything about myself." What they really mean is, "I just want to advertise my business" and that's a big mistake. People don't network with your business, they network with you! People do business with people. When people KNOW, LIKE and TRUST you, they are comfortable doing business with YOUR business!

People connect through emotions and life events. Connections can start with family, friends, business partners and your kids' friends' parents. The strongest connections come through shared interests: kids, pets, high school or college, church, music, movies, or something else that carries a strong emotional component. Relationships devoid of passion and emotion remain merely transactional. Think of the difference between buying a cup of coffee from McDonald's or your friendly neighborhood barista.

Social networking: what's in it for you? My friend and mentor Al Ritter, a business coach who works with the best of the best, generously gives me time and advice while expecting nothing in return. People like him and your relationships with them are your greatest assets in business. Think about it: Your best customers recommend you because they believe in you and evangelize—spread the good word about—your efforts.

Building personal relationships is the cornerstone of building your business! Yes, relationships demand commitment, but you need to make the time to help others without expectation of reciprocation. Invest in your connections by serving as a resource or a sounding board, but mostly by being a friend.

I know this relational model may be the antithesis of what you've learned about building a brand... but in a small- to medium-sized business, relationships are price-less! Do the hard work of building relationships through your business page, by educating, informing and enter-taining and you earn the interest, respect and gift of their time from your connections. Being yourself and connecting on a real and emotional level helps you create lasting relationships, referral partners, evangelists and, eventually, more business.

Being you, human and accessible, takes effort and may involve taking risks... but it's what people have come to expect, so get posting! Then, when your connections share a great blog, an article, or a funny picture you post, you expand your audience and your influence grows.

CHAPTER 15: WHO ARE YOU TALKING TO?

BACON-IZMS

- Know who you're talking to and what they want to hear

- You communicate to many groups of people

- Use different strategies to communicate with each group

- People communicate the way they like to be communicated to

- Be where your clients want to communicate with you

Know your target audience and what they need

After getting inspired by a presentation or webinar, people tend to dive into social networking without knowing the most basic thing: who they want or need to communicate with. Often they need to communicate to multiple audiences and don't realize they can't use a "One Size Fits All" solution (even though some gurus try to tell you that their favorite social media tool can be the only one you need to use).

You communicate to more than one group of people

The best example I use comes from working with nonprofits. They work with what I like to call silos. Yes, like the storage unit used on a farm. Now I am no farmer, but I know that you have different silos for corn, wheat and soy.

Many nonprofits try the "One Size Fits All" approach to their communication strategy. They hope to reach enough of an audience to make a difference using just a printed newsletter, or only a Facebook Page. They fail to realize that they also have multiple distinct audience "silos" that they need to be filling with information. Let's take a look at the average nonprofit's multiple audiences.

Donors. First off, the lifeblood of any nonprofit is funding. Most that I have worked with still rely heavily on individual donations, even those funded by federal, state or local grants. Donors for many, especially long-established charities, tend to be older folks, people who have sufficient discretionary funds to support the causes near and dear to their hearts.

Both my wife's mother and my own died of breast cancer. We are both pet lovers who have adopted dogs from rescues. Some of our closest friends have autistic children. I was once homeless. All of us support organizations with which we have an emotional and life connection, so you can guess that we give our time and resources to groups helping pets in need, homeless people, and autism and cancer research.

When nonprofits approach older donors, they need to recognize that these donors may tend to be a little less electronically savvy as a group. My wife and I personify the intersection of that technological divide. While we are both computer savvy, I tend to lean more to the geek side.

If you want to reach my wife, you send her a printed newsletter, with stories and pictures and she will sit down and read it cover to cover. If you send her an email newsletter, it might well get lost in the abyss of her inbox.

On the other hand, I appreciate a short email with links to a website, so I can click on and read a story that interested me. If you send me a paper newsletter, it ends up on a pile on my desk... and more often than not in the recycle bin weeks later, still unread.

Note that I'm saying send newsletters. Donors like to know that their funds are being used wisely and how they intended their donation to be used. They like feel-good success stories, testimonials and news that they can relate to. Unfortunately, some nonprofits think that they only need to send out that end of the year "Ask" envelope for the money to pour in like it has in the past. In reality, similar organizations that are court those same donors have gotten more diligent and strategic about their marketing communications.

In fact, donors comprise only the first of the many audiences a nonprofit needs to contact. But even thinking only about reaching donors, organizations may need to use not only quarterly print newsletters but monthly email blasts and weekly blog posts, along with daily Facebook posts, to reach the wide variety of people with interests in the organization and its messages.

Volunteers. The other lifeblood of nonprofits is people willing to donate their time. Nearly all non-profits count on volunteers to help, if only to paint a room, clean up a flower bed, do some filing or perform any other office or maintenance tasks needed to help offset the limitations of shrinking budgets and reduced staff. Some organizations also depend on volunteers to perform their core mission.

At the Hesed House homeless shelter in Aurora, IL, waves of volunteers help feed and care for the least, last and lost. With a staff of 50, they organize more than 500 volunteers per month to help serve more than 1000 homeless or near-homeless people a year.

More often than not, volunteers are teens and twenty-somethings, people who have more time than money. In fact, the Millennials, whether Gen Y or Gen X, feel it's their calling to get their hands dirty rather than pull out their checkbooks.

If you want to communicate service opportunities t to that group, a print newsletter might as well be a stone tablet. Even email is passé to this group. Text them.

If you tell them about an event a month out, you may get a few takers. If you tell them a week out, you get more. Go ahead and send the advance notices, but also send texts or tweets just a day or two before, or even the morning of your event, to get the greatest response from Millenials, who live for today (or maybe this weekend).

Also, if you text or tweet to your volunteers, you have a much better chance of them sharing that text with their friends, gaining your organization some tag-along volunteers.

Nonprofits realize that volunteers often turn into committee members. Committee members sometimes turn into board members and likely grow into donors as well. Board members sometimes become fundraisers as well as donors. Leaders understand that, for an organization to grow, it must nurture and embrace this progression from volunteer to donor and leader and fundraiser. If not, the organization runs the risk of shrinking or, even worse, becoming irrelevant.

Those In need. The people a nonprofit serves constitute the most elusive and transitory group with which the organization needs to communicate. The people needing a nonprofit's help might be in hiding because of abuse, protected by HIPA laws, just plain shy—or they may not have access to mainstream media or the internet. That means you may have to rely on liaison with other agencies, or government organizations to communicate your messages. You might also need to use posters, emails, LinkedIn, Twitter, even public presentations.

You communicate to many groups of people

Each organization has its own audiences and communication DNA. The point is, your business also has multiple audiences. You probably need to give different information and advice to new people you meet, current clients, past clients, vendors and suppliers. It really helps the success of your communication plans if you can get some idea what the age range, technological prowess and expectations are for each audience.

Sit back and take stock of your tools, messages, methods and audiences. What could work for you with the audiences your business wants to reach?

Not every person will respond to one, two, or even three of these message methodologies. You may need to apply multiple methods to reach everyone in a target group. And remember, measurement is king. You have to monitor and asses what's working, what's trending and what's slowly (or quickly) failing.

I hope this shows you that you need audience evaluation, a plan, and an ability to use face-to-face networking, social networking and multiple communication media, monitored through measurement and evaluation, to succeed.

People communicate the way they like to be communicated to

Face it, we are creatures of habit and we like to be comfortable. If you are younger, then you probably spend a lot of time texting and tweeting on your smart phone. If you are older, you may spend a lot more time talking on the phone than you do texting or posting and commenting in Facebook.

We all tend to communicate with the technology we feel most comfortable with. This means we also respond more readily when contacted through the technology we use the most.

The point is, you need to be where your customers or potential customers ARE, not where you want them to be.

Not a day that goes by but I have customers reach out to me with posts, groups or direct messages on Facebook, LinkedIn, and Twitter, emails, texts, phone calls and voice mails, and more. I even have a link on my contact page to my Native American name, in case someone wants to use smoke signals!

Be where your clients want to communicate with you

You need to be wherever clients or customers want to communicate with you. If you're not there, you will certainly miss potential business. If you are not responding to them everywhere they go to ask for information or help, you can rest assured that some or all of your competition is and will!

So, you take the first step and set up the accounts. Your next step involves monitoring them on a regular basis. This does not mean you have to spend all day glued to the internet. If you have a smart phone, it can alert you to any and all messages. You can also use online tools such as Hootsuite to monitor all of your accounts in one nice, neat package.

So what do you do besides monitoring these accounts? Make sure you don't try a one-size-fits-all campaign. Remember that different tools and methodologies will communicate better with some silos (new or current customers) than others (past customers and other contacts). Don't forget to contact power partners and vendors, either. Create separate campaigns just to keep them informed.

Finally, make sure you have a presence in all the places where your customers and potential customers want to find you, not just where you are comfortable being. Those spaces, tools and technologies are changing all the time, so stay on top of the changes. You customers will make it perfectly clear by what social media tools they use to try to get a hold of you! Be There!

CHAPTER 16:
GETTING SOCIAL

BACON-IZMS

- Social networking is a process not an advertisement

- Post content that engages your audience

- Provide interesting useful information

- Find fun content to entertain and engage your audience

- Educate: Teaching positions you as an expert

- Post content that followers will want to share

- Social networking is all about people

Social networking is a process not an advertisement

Social networking, like its partner relationship marketing, is a process. It takes all the things we do on a daily basis as business owners, vendors or employees and forms how we do them into an executable plan with measurable results. Both start with relationships first and only add marketing after good relationships have been established.

Remember what I told you about ME-dia? I am sure you have seen people who treat social networking like little kids view a trip to Chuck-E-Cheese. Kids keep throwing tokens into the machines to earn as many tickets as they can because they can cash the tickets in for trashy little trinkets. You know you could have bought 10 (or more) of whatever your kids choose for the money they spent to win the tickets they traded in!

That's how some people treat social networking. They try to gather as many followers as possible so they have a huge audience for their broadcast sales messages. Then they trade on their relationships for a few sales. Trust me, people know when they are being used, treated like paper tickets.

Can you really build relationships with hundreds or thousands of people? That depends on who you are and what you have to offer, but consider carefully, are you using social ME-dia or are you social networking?

Social ME-dia efforts focus on you and not others. That, my friends, is advertising not relationship marketing. Let me explain...

Most celebrities do one-way contact. They post and people follow. Many celebrities have millions of followers but follow only a few. Tiger Woods has 3 million Twitter followers but follows only 17. Ashton Kutcher has 14 million followers and follows around 700 people. Oprah has more than 17 million followers but follows about 100 people. No one has time to build lasting relationships with 17 million people, do they? That is Social ME-dia!

What celebrities do works for them because they don't need to build true relationships with you... you already know who they are and admire something that they do.

So they just need to get their message out to you: go see my movie, buy my album, read my book, come watch me play. Of course, to keep their followers, they need to do even this outbound messaging in an appealing way.

But actual social networking involves networking—creating connections—as well as using online social communication tools. Social networking works as an extension of your face-to-face networking. You continue online relationships that you made in person. You can network one-to-one through email, Facebook or LinkedIn messages and private tweets, or one-to-many, but you should never broadcast messages that do not invite interaction on social media.

No rule says someone who has hundreds or thousands of followers is just a broadcaster. They may truly be very popular because they often post relevant and useful information. But, in my experience, you'll find many more Social ME-dia people with lots of followers, than social networkers. Producing Social ME-dia is easy. Social networking takes lots more planning and work.

At this time, the average number of followers for a business or person stacks up like this:

Facebook profile	200+
Facebook business page	100+
Twitter account	200+
LinkedIn profile	150+

You can find other numbers for all of these, but these reflect spot on what I've seen helping many clients with their accounts.

In business, I think you have a better chance of knowing 100-200 people personally than thousands. Exceptions would include those who work all over the country or world, especially those who travel for that work.

So, who are your business contacts? Look at your address book and your Quickbooks records or whatever accounting system you use. Chances are you have 250-500 people in your address book and 50-150 clients in your billing records. If you have been in business longer, you'll likely have more people in your proto-network. If your business is very small or very new, you'll have fewer people on these lists.

Post content that engages your audience

The person with the most contacts does not win a prize. Number of friends, likes or fans is only measured by those who want to boast of more contacts. But a contact alone is worth nothing. The real prize comes to those who create the most interactions with the contacts they already have. These interactions sometimes gain them additional followers, usually lead to more interpersonal interactions and will ultimately bring in sales.

Social networking sites like Klout.com do not measure the number of people you have in your network, they measure the engagement of the contacts in your network. Granted, those who have more contacts can more easily create more engagement and win higher scores. However, many people and businesses with more contacts than you may have lower scores because they generate less engagement.

I have seen many so-called gurus of social media who post and post and post, but get few or no likes, no comments and no shares. Engagement is measured by interaction, not posting frequency.

This means that logic should tell you that the number of people in your network is nowhere near as important as the number of people who actively respond by liking, commenting and sharing your posts. Tracking engagement on competitors' social media serves as a good gauge of how successful your competition's posts are. The more engaged their followers (no matter how many followers they have), the better job they are doing at social networking.

Provide interesting useful information

You grab your coffee in the morning, boot up your computer and log into your social media of choice saying, "I can't wait to read all the ads I've been missing." I don't think so. Who has nothing better to do than wade through 100 spam emails? Or a Facebook news feed or Twitter feed filled with fabulous offers? Honestly? You HATE that! Then why would you think this is a good strategy for your business?

People log into social networking for many reasons. They want to:

- Keep up with relevant news

- Maintain important relationships

- Get entertained

- Stay informed

- Be educated

- Be moved by compassionate or controversial comments or memes

- Find conversations

... but NEVER to be sold. That's Google's job.

Some of the most beloved brands on Facebook get this. Follow Dunkin Donuts. Yes, they post special offers, but in the context of a page with 'Fan of the Week' picture contests where they give away their products. Did I mention pictures? Lots of pictures, pictures that get thousands of likes and hundreds of comments and shares. Dunkin Donuts isn't selling, it's engaging, which promote sales.

In the late '90s, the programming on cable channels like History, Discovery and Biography spawned the term "infotainment," meaning information wrapped in entertainment. That trend has warped into reality TV shows like "Pawn Stars" home remodeling shows, "Real" housewives and others. Think of social media as reality TV on steroids.

Twitter is where most of the world's news stories now break first. The deaths of Michael Jackson and Whitney Houston brought more than 1000 tweets per second. Same with revolution in Egypt or fighting in Syria. Live reporting and commentary no longer mean what you watch what Walter Cronkite or Peter Jennings have to say on TV during the evening news. People tune into Twitter, Facebook and other social media for the news of the day, all day, as it happens.

Unlike in the day of Cronkite and Jennings, this means the news thus reported get little journalistic vetting or source-checking. But you get lots of commentary, unregulated and unrelenting. Stories break so fast that facts often get distorted and flat out false reports get spread. That's part of what makes social media so hard for people used to traditional print, radio and TV news to KNOW, LIKE AND TRUST. At the same time, this imme-diacy makes internet-based news hugely alluring to those people who didn't grow up depending on traditional news media.

Educate your audience: Teaching positions you as an industry expert

Another way that you create conversations is being the purveyor of great information. What I mean by this is, you find interesting articles on the web and share them on your social networks. Depending on your business or industry, you can find dozens, if not thousands, of sources on the web that aggregate great information you can share. You can start with these:

- technorati.com, a website that collects and rates blogs based on relevance and content, helps you search for blogs that may give you daily tips or information that your audience will appreciate.

- stumbleupon.com. You choose a topic and this site will show web pages that help you explore the topics you choose.

- Reddit.com, an online community where you can ask questions and get answers, lets users promote trending topics by voting for them.

Google Alerts offers simple and effective way to have information that you can share delivered. Go to Google.com/alerts to set up an alert to be emailed to you as it happens, daily or weekly. Not only can you and should you set up alerts for your name and your business, to be sent as they crop up, but you can pick any other topic and have it mailed to you daily. I have alerts set up for Facebook and LinkedIn. They send me a daily digest of news on those topics that happened in the past 24 hours.

How do you know what and when to post? Ask your followers what they want. Also, pay attention to what they have liked, commented on or shared. Followers will make sure you know what they like and don't by whether they engage with or ignore your posts.

One of the most effective ways to communicate and build your brand online is to blog. Blog, short for web log, was originally a fairly geeky thing to do. Today, blogs have transformed into incredibly mainstream tools, easy to set up and use. (more about this in Chapter 26).

A blog allows you to create content for your followers. You can teach them tips and techniques associated with what you do. If people like what you post, they will interact with you through comments. Even better, they may share or repost your blog for all of their followers to see, thus greatly extending your online reach.

Post content that followers will want to share

One of the key things that makes social networking different from other sources of promotion or advertising is the ability of posts to go viral. What does that mean?

Remember the cartoon I mentioned posting, "Amazing Grease, How Sweet the Sound that Saved a Wrench Like Me!" The page on which I posted it has only 300+ fans, but the cartoon got shared more than 1,000 times, garnering views by more than 100,000 people. Social networking going viral can do that for you. But for that to happen, you have to produce something that your audience loves and wants to share and that their friends and friends of friends may share as well. So one person shares, and 10 of their friends share, and 10 of THEIR friends share, and 10 more of THEIR friends share... and voila, you have a 1,000 shares.

Now keep in mind that Facebook puts the brakes on your posts by only showing them to about 20% of your audience. They started something called promoted posts in hopes that you would be willing to pay $5 or more to have all your fans see all your posts. That means that only 60 of my 300 fans originally saw this. But my post still got viewed by more than 100,000 people. That's the real power of going viral.

This was truly catching lightning in a bottle and it really opened my eyes to how remarkably going viral can work. It happens all the time with silly videos on YouTube. Some of the people who create viral videos end up on morning television news shows. It could happen with your business as well... as long as you take the time and make the effort to create original material that your fans feel is worth sharing.

In sum, being social is about being human. You need to know what your audience is interested in, interact with your connections, constantly ask them what they want and measure the results. Social ME-dia is when you only post hard-sell posts about your business. Social networking is all about them, your audience.

Becoming a trusted source takes time and commitment. Social networking is a communications tool, not an advertising methodology. Make sure you respect people's time and attention by making your posts interesting. With luck, you too may catch lightning in a bottle!

Social networking is all about people

Social networking is about people... people who can care and share. The people on social networks want to be educated with information that can help them. They like inspirational quotes, pictures, jokes, answers to their questions, prayers for their problems and to be treated like friends, not prospects. Producing or providing content that they like can produce sharing and connectivity results far beyond anything you could imagine!

CHAPTER 17: CREATIVE RIGHTS AND WRONGS

BACON-IZMS

- Companies make money off your innocent mistakes

- You can't just copy and paste images, text or videos

- Understand copyright rights and wrongs

- Protect yourself by using paid-for services

- Understand Fair Use and Creative Commons

- If you'll profit from someone else's work, pay or beware

Companies make money off your innocent mistakes

Now that we're discussing content, you need to be aware of the legal issues that could affect your choice of what to post and how.

Back in the days when I owned my recording studio, one of our profit centers involved selling on-hold music systems. We also produced the loops people would hear when you called a company and were put on hold, mini-commercials with library background music that we licensed from legitimate music libraries. We paid thousands of dollars a year to have the rights to use and distribute this music in radio and TV commercials, video productions and the on-hold systems.

Before the days of the big record companies suing the likes of Napster and college kids sharing music online, the major music licensing agencies, ASCAP and BMI acted as the music police. They would go into bars and night-clubs, making them buy performance licenses to pay the writers and performers of copyrighted music. With those licenses, DJs and cover bands who made maybe $250 a night could play "Sweet Home Alabama" and "Takin' Care of Business" all night long. ASCAP and BMI knew the bands had no money, so they strong-armed the owners of the venues where the bands or DJs played.

That's also what made our on-hold business tick. ASCAP and BMI would do the same thing to companies who simply connected local radio stations to the on-hold systems built into their phone system. ASCAP and BMI would call businesses and ask to be placed on hold. If they heard copyrighted music, they would send the company a bill for $150,000. Only after the business agreed to a licensing deal and penalties could those charges be negotiated.

You can't just copy and paste images, text or videos

Populating a website with text, links, photos and video can become the internet equivalent of music on hold for your business. Companies who own copyrights to content and images patrol for people who infringe on their copyright to supplement lost income from unlicensed use!

Because I run my own business, I receive endless offers to buy this service or that product. One day, I received a FedEx envelope from a stock image company. I assumed it was just another solicitation because I have often used, and paid for use of, stock images. After a few days, I finally opened it. I found a bill for $12,000 for back compensation for an image. Needless to say, I was caught completely off guard.

Companies such as Masterfile and Getty Images employ third-party companies to scan the internet for unlicensed uses of their images. They use tools like "The Way Back Machine" (archive.org) to view versions of websites that may be 10 years old or older. How do I know this? From the experience of calling to dispute this bill. The stock image company explained that they'd found one of their images on my website. They said it had been there for six years and their licensing fee was $2000 a year. I told them there was no way... but they were right. I'd put up a temporary page on my website with a placeholder graphic from a disc I had lying around. I'd had no idea what it was from, but the image looked cool. I'd never intended the page to go live on my final website, but the page and that graphic were still out on the 'net.

I tried to argue that it was a rogue page and not part of any real marketing or money-making activities, but they said it didn't matter. It was out there and they found it, so the bill was valid. Then they started sending emails with PDFs of cases where they'd won $100,000 copyright judgments in courts. They said I had no recourse but to pay the bill. I don't know about you, but I did not have an extra $12,000 lying around doing nothing.

Panic-stricken and distraught, I consulted a lawyer. After months of going back and forth, I settled with the stock photo company. Learning my big lesson cost me thousands of dollars, although less than the original bill, to my relief. I'd already known that publishing unlicensed content to the internet could be a copyright infringement, but this one blindsided me because my infringement was completely unintentional.

So, having been burned once, I researched this subject like crazy and found out that the investigation to which I'd fallen prey is common practice. If these multinational companies cannot make money selling people $2,000-a-year images, they will chase down people who did not even know they're breaking laws and sue them.

I have also seen some clients falling victim to the uptick in this kind of investigation. My clients have worked with companies that used random images to create a website for them. The stock photo giants don't try to track down and sue the vendor, they sue the company whose name is on the website.

All that needs to happen for this complaint to go away is for the vendor to show it legitimately paid for the stock photo or content, but sometimes the design firms have hired interns or developers who do not know or care about copyright laws and have long since moved on from the firm. Because you are now a past client and not a current payment source, the firm may have no desire to take responsibility. This often leaves you, as the website domain owner, holding the bag.

Understand copyright rights and wrongs

When it comes to your website, ebooks, or anything you publish or communicate online, you need to know about copyright laws and how they can affect you and your business.

First off, nothing replaces having a good lawyer when you need one, or having the right insurance before you need it.

If you produce materials for others, you should have a good contract in place that spells out your and your client's responsibilities when it comes to arranging and paying for copyrights. When I owned my recording studio, some clients would demand that I use copyrighted songs for their videos, promos for meetings and the like. I would make them sign a waiver, claiming full responsibility for using that music and accepting 100% responsibility if they ever were sued. Was that a 100% guarantee that I would remain in the clear? No way, but it made some clients think twice. Luckily, I was never pulled into a legal battle over copyrighted materials.

Secondly, you cannot just pull images off the internet to use on your website or in your blogs. It's so easy: you search a topic in Google, click the image tab and find hundreds, if not thousands, of lovely images. Can you grab them? Yes. Is that legal? Probably not!

Some people think that photo-sharing sites like Flickr and Instagram are fair game for grabbing and using photos, but nothing could be further from the truth. Many professional photographers use these sites to market their businesses, and they maintain copyrights on their materials.

Protect yourself by using paid-for services

You really only have two choices: create images yourself, or pay for them. You can find dozens of affordable stock image companies online. Two of my favorites, IStockPhoto.com and ShutterStock.com, offer either pay-as–you-go credit plans, or yearly licensing deals.

Make sure you read the licensing agreements carefully either way. Often they set boundaries on how and how often you can use their photos.

The biggest benefit to you from purchasing art is the paper trail you get. Your online account usually shows the history of purchases made. So, if someone accuses you of copyright infringement, you can produce a receipt of your purchase and the agreement.

Understand Fair Use and Creative Commons

I hope I have not scared you away from using images in your website and blog. Still photos and video drastically improve web traffic and measurably improve a viewer's impression of your materials.

I am not a lawyer (although I have played one in radio commercials), but I can tell you about some best practices I've run into. Be aware, I work in Illinois and the laws may vary from state to state, so you should consult a local lawyer before implementing any sharing of materials created by someone else.

You can do two things that with relative confidence: share links and use a Creative Commons License.

Fair use: A portion of copyright law, under the category of "Fair Use," exists to allows you to copy and paste images and content under specific conditions.

A website post by the Stanford University Libraries and Academic Information Resources describes Fair Use:

> In its most general sense, a fair use is any copying of copyrighted material done for a limited and "trans-formative" purpose, such as to comment upon, criticize, or parody a copyrighted work. Such uses can be done without permission from the copyright

owner. In other words, fair use is a defense against a claim of copyright infringement. If your use qualifies as a fair use, then it would not be considered an illegal infringement.

So what is a "transformative" use? If this definition seems ambiguous or vague, be aware that millions of dollars in legal fees have been spent attempting to define what qualifies as a fair use. There are no hard-and-fast rules, only general rules and varied court decisions, because the judges and lawmakers who created the fair use exception did not want to limit its definition. Like free speech, they wanted it to have an expansive meaning that could be open to interpretation.

Most fair use analysis falls into two categories: (1) commentary and criticism, or (2) parody.

Now keep in mind that some social media networks, like Facebook, fall under the Fair Use statute since posts there qualify as personal commentary, although that may not hold on pages for business use. Use in your blog may or may not qualify as Fair use depending on the blog's purpose (business, political, etc.). Also, some rumblings have surfaced about other social media networks, like Pinterest, stating that responsibility for legitimate use of text and images rests on the person posting content. Pinterest has made that this policy to separate it from any legal ramifications of what users post or pin.

Creative Commons licenses: Wikipedia tells us:

Creative Commons (CC) is a non-profit organization headquartered in Mountain View, California, United States devoted to expanding the range of creative works available for others to build upon legally and to share. The organization has released several copyright licenses, known as Creative Commons licenses, free of charge to the public. These licenses allow creators to communicate which rights they reserve and which rights they waive for the benefit of recipients or other creators. An easy to understand one-page explanation of rights, with associated visual symbols, explains the specifics of each Creative Commons license. Creative Commons licenses do not replace copyright, but are based upon it.

Link sharing gets you around the copyright restriction against copying and pasting text or pictures from an online website. Unless otherwise noted, copying and pasting a link to an entire article is not only legal, it's generally encouraged. You are driving traffic back to the website or blog at the link you're posting and thus helping them. That's why websites like LinkedIn, Facebook and others let you share links outside of their properties. YouTube has a 'Share' feature built into almost every video. They WANT you to share their content because that drives more traffic back to them.

Back-linking is also good for search engine optimization. The more people link back to your website, the more the search engines consider you credible, so again, your links help the other person's website.

When it comes to linking to images, a right click on the image lets you copy the URL. When you paste the URL into Facebook, or even your blog, you are not copying and pasting the image into the property, just a link to it. This is not a failsafe way to use images from other websites, but linking is much less likely to get you in hot water than copy and paste because it preserves the origin of the image.

If you'll profit from someone else's work, pay or beware

The bottom line here is that people offering a Creative Commons license may give you rights to use their content on social media, but not as a tool for direct selling, like it probably would when used be within your website.

So before you sign up for any social media account, read the user agreement. And if you think you run ANY chance of copyright infringement with text or images you'd like to use, DON'T!

Insurance: If you post, create content, blog, or do anything on the internet, it makes sense to get the right insurance to help you avoid disastrous liability. Some small businesses think that just getting a million dollar umbrella policy will cover them for all business issues, but they are wrong.

You want a specific kind of policy called Errors and Omissions, or E&O, insurance, which is designed to protect you in cases where you did not intend wrong but erred by ignorance or accident. You cannot buy E&O insurance after the fact and it does not protect you from blatant copyright infringement, but it can be money well spent if you find yourself caught up in a situation where you did not intend to defraud or unknowingly crossed the wrong lines. Contact a business insurance professional in your area to learn more.

After my run-in with the stock photo company, you can bet I bought an E&O policy as soon as I'd paid off the settlement and my lawyer!

I don't want to scare you, but before I start talking about using social networks to promote your brand and business, you need to know what you should and should not do! 'Free Speech' is not the same as repurposing content with a for-profit purpose. Copyright laws mostly protect those who can afford to enforce it, so be aware, be safe and protect yourself. You don't want to get one of those $12,000 (or larger!) bills delivered by FedEx.

CHAPTER 18:
UNDER THE SEA

BACON-IZMS

- You can run, but you can't hide (from the internet)

- Go with the flow, don't fight the tide

- YOU have to manage your own reputation

- DON'T hide your contact information

- Be yourself, not just your business

You can run, but you can't hide (from the internet)

I constantly hear people say they want to get active on social media but don't want to set up a personal profile. What they mean is, "I'm fine with post messages about our company, but I don't want anyone to know who I am or what I ate for lunch, or see pictures of my cat!"

I can understand a regional, national or international company not feeling the need to show a personal side. But if you run a local business, why would you want to be anonymous?

I also thoroughly understand the desire to separate your personal life and business life, but the internet has already started blurring that line more every day, whatever you do!

Don't believe me? If you need proof, just Google yourself. What you will find is either a blessing or a curse! If you are trying to protect your identity, you may be appalled about how much information is already out there. But if you are trying to promote yourself over the internet, then you will find whether and how other people find you... or your competitors (or people with the same name as you).

There is no turning back time or turning the internet off. Websites like whitepages.com have your address and phone number. Others, like zillow.com, can tell people what your house is worth. Countless websites can give more detail about your life than you probably care to know.

Go with the flow, don't fight the tide

In this New Reality, you must (and you should) protect specific private personal identity data like your Social Security or credit card numbers and medical records, but any public information is already out on the internet. There is no going back. So I ask you, would you not do better to embrace change?

I grew up in New York, taking summer trips to the Jersey Shore and Long Island. My brother and sister were local swimming champions. I went swimming in the ocean so many times that I felt I knew it like a family member. I had much respect for and at the same time little fear of water.

I was about 10 when my family vacationed in Florida. I went playing in the water as I had done dozens, if not hundreds of times before. Waves came in and out as I frolicked. Then, all of a sudden, one wave flowed in a little stronger. The next thing I know, the water had swept my feet out from under me and I was being carried out into the ocean. I never had a chance to take a breath, it felt like and the more I fought, the harder I was being pulled under and away from the shore. I felt terrified but I finally stopped fighting back. I decided to go with the flow because I really had no choice. But once I went with the flow, I regained my buoyancy, managed to get to the surface, rode out the rip current and swam back to shore.

So you can either fight change and lose your chance to use the internet, or embrace change and profit from what social networking has to offer. People will certainly research you on LinkedIn, Facebook and Google. If you go with the flow, you can post positive, relevant information to enhance your online brand. You can position yourself way ahead of the game if you manage your online reputation rather than letting the internet manage it for you, so go with the flow!

YOU have to manage your own reputation

I have had more than one customer ask me how to remove negative posts or information about them from Google. The answer to that is not simple. The site with the most traffic and the highest reputation always wins. The best thing you can do is to do your best to push the negative content further down Google searches by providing positive content that outranks the bad stuff. Social networking sites such as LinkedIn, Facebook and Twitter provide good places to start.

Another thing you can do is get connected with PR request sites like HARO (Help a Reporter Out) and Reporter Connection. If you become a source that provides content, you can get interviews with popular magazines, news outlets, other websites, blogs and more. These websites will send you daily or multiple daily

requests for expertise and commentary. You get no guar-
antees that anyone will interview you or use your content,
but the more you respond to opportunities, the better
your chances become.

I have been interviewed for radio shows all over the
country. I have been included in webinars and podcasts,
and I have been featured in blogs, news stories and even
national magazines because I've answered requests from
these and other websites. Needless to say, some of these
well-respected and heavy-hitting resources associated
my name with high-ranking Google searches.

These press contacts are interviewing you, not your
business. This is why managing your personal brand
matters. Even though your business name may show
up, your personal name draws more weight in Google
searches and may provide you a better opportunity to
push negative content down the list.

DON'T hide your contact information

Business people and consumers alike are sick and tired of
companies trying to redirect you away from talking to a
human. Not too long ago, tech companies like Microsoft
and Hewlett Packard thought using call centers in India to
handle their tech support was a good idea. After all, they
could pay people pennies to do the same job that would
cost hundreds of dollars to have people do in the US.

Nothing embodies frustration like trying to get tech
support from someone who barely speaks English, works
from a script and may never have seen the product or
software you're calling about. Someone would answer
the phone and guide you through a script in hopes of
solving your problem. In my experience, it took you,
the customer two to three times longer to solve your
problem than if you'd been able to talk to someone

knowledgeable who understood spoken English, but the companies saved big bucks on tech support for products you'd already paid for. They'd decided that saving money was more important than keeping potential repeat customers happy.

Companies continue to play hide and seek with their contact information. In some cases, it's more like a scavenger hunt. If you go to point A, then back up to point D, and navigate back to points B and C, they may give you access to a "Submit A Ticket" form. You might then wait days to get a simple, cryptic answer. Or you can play Tech Support Roulette until you get the right answer... or simply give up.

Some companies try to avoid talking with you even when you do finally find a phone number and actually call in, by greeting you with messages directing you to tools on the internet: knowledge bases, support tickets, or instant message chat (so you cannot hear foreign accents). Then, after entering appropriate numbers on 4 to 8 menus, you may earn the opportunity to talk with an actual human. But, if you get escalated to level 2 or level 3, you get more hold time, more questions, even starting over and repeating all your information.

Google is worth hundreds of dollars a share. They will call you to sell you Adwords (that's how they make their bundles of money), but do they give you a tech support number? No, just tons of online knowledge bases and video training.

Apple redefined technical support for tech companies. Many others have started to follow suit (see Microsoft Stores). Apple changed the face of tech support, literally. When they opened Apple Stores in cities and towns all across the country, they put customers first with people who greet you when you walk in. Their Genius Bar lets you can schedule an appointment online to meet with an expert face to face. The experts will do their best to solve your problem, answer questions and teach you how to fix similar problems yourself. Which system would you rather deal with?

Now, this is not a tech support book, but imagine your customers or potential customers having to go through the old-model vs. Apple type tech support to get to your company. Which experience would you rather give them?

If you part of a larger business, I thoroughly understand that you face a much harder situation acting as an individual on the internet. However, as I have mentioned before, B2B (business to business) and B2C (business to consumer) are fictions. All business is P2P (people to people).

Be yourself, not just your business

So you want to create a social networking profile to handle info, support, or whatever for your business. First, ask yourself, who would YOU want to talk to? Faceless Tech Support or Ben, Mary or Fredrick? Tech support and sales are as much a part of your brand as your logo.

The companies that score the biggest success with social media generally have a single person that manages messages, is recognizable to users and is accountable for the process. If people feel that they are talking to a machine, they feel devalued. If they know they are talking with a real person, you get an emotional connection with users that can help build your business and your brand.

Another common mistake I see is people who are not comfortable with social networking or online tools, just handing the job over to a 20-something niece, nephew, random kid or employee. Ask yourself, If your customers are 40 to 60 years old, do you really want a 20-something to be the voice of your company?

Can you really trust them to stay on brand or understand the questions, problems and issues your customer audience faces?

Going with the flow reflects caring what your clients want more than what you want. It's Not About You... it's about your customers and potential customers. Playing hide and seek with support only frustrates people. Hiding behind a company shroud and not being a real person does not make you look like a bigger company, it just make you look like a company that does not care.

Relationship marketing goes way beyond social networking, it gets to the core of making people feel valued, important and special. The biggest point here is, know who you are talking to... who is talking to them... and who your client or potential client wants to communicate with. Just go with the flow!

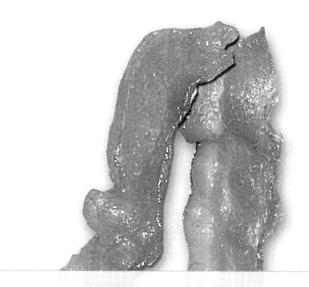

PART 4: TOOLS OF THE TRADE

I f you are hoping I am going to tell you how to set up a Facebook Business page or a Twitter account, sorry. This section (indeed, this whole book) is more about the whys than the hows of social media networking.

Now that we have the KNOW, LIKE AND TRUST parts of the networking equation defined, we need to examine the techniques and tools that make this philosophy tick: how will you engage with people and what do they do when they engage with you.

As I've explained before, getting your contacts and connections to your home base is your ultimate goal. We will explore what that means for the various social media in terms of best practices and to maximize your return on investment in time and their ROI in trust!

No one right answer exists that tells which social networking site will work best for you. You learned about communicating differently with different groups using the metaphor of silos. We'll revisit that metaphor to look at each social network as part of different silos' optimal communication methods.

More importantly, you have to get out of your comfort zone and learn where the people who you want to communicate with spend their time!

CHAPTER 19: FACEBOOK

BACON-IZMS

- Facebook has over 1 billion followers

- Your own and your business personalities on Facebook

- Relationships start by being you, not just your business

- Create interactions by pictures and blog posts

- You can interact as yourself or your business

- Business pages offer analytics and multiple landing pages

Facebook started as a way for male college students to connect with girls. If you have not seen the movie The Social Network, I recommend it... but back to using Facebook. It has morphed from a college age-only website to one where kids are leaving in droves because their parents and grandparents have joined.

Facebook has more than 1 billion followers

It has grown up and grown in general. More than one billion people now have accounts on Facebook. People log in to connect with friends and family. When news and events happen, they log in for comfort and reassurance, to comment, or to converse.

Some people just play games, while others want nothing to do with those. Millions of pictures and images get posted each day. Some are personal, some political and others are memes or jokes. You can find links to news, blogs, inspirational quotes and much more on Facebook.

I have been to countless seminars and webinars where presenters promise your business a billion person audience on Facebook. But remember, not all of those billion Facebook users speak English. In fact, only about 168 million of them live in the US. Factor in the users who would not be interested in your products and services and you find a much narrower field of dreams. Finally, if you run a local business, how many people live within your market area? And of those, how many will buy or need what you sell? How many other companies compete for that piece of the pie?

The average business page gets between 100 and 250 likes. This may not sound like a lot, but even at that level, if some posts go viral, your reach may expand to thousands. What matters most is that you get in the game.

I was asked to talk at a Pella Windows regional convention at Soldier Field in Chicago. As I was setting up, dozens of remodelers started piling into the room. A few of these men, primarily 40 to 60 years old, came up to me and said, "I am not sure why I am here. I don't care where anybody went for dinner and I certainly don't want to see pictures of someone's pet!" After I finished setting up, I spent the next hour or so explaining the finer points of using social media to grow their businesses. I finished with this offer, "What if I could introduce you to thousands of 40- to 60-year old women in your town, women who have a disposable income of more than $100,000, who have to keep their homes because of the housing bubble and want to remodel their kitchens, bathrooms or basements? If you would like me to introduce you to them, raise your hands." Every person in the room enthusiastically obliged. Then I gave them the hard new, saying, "They are all on Facebook!"

Your own and your business personalities on Facebook

In the Facebook world, you have two personas. Facebook calls your personal side your profile. People can "friend" you or subscribe to your posts through your profile page.

If people ask to "friend" you—to connect as your friends—you can choose whether you approve each request. If a Facebook friend gets too annoying, you can choose to hide all posts but keep that person as a friend (so that person can still see your posts), or you may choose to de-friend them, cutting off the connection.

Others—people you have not accepted as friends and who you may not even know—have the option of subscribing. That lets them read your posts without being able to comment or like them. Subscribers also cannot post anything on your timeline. Facebook added the subscribe option because the 5000-friend limit frustrated celebrities who wanted Facebook exposure but didn't want to use a business page.

The second persona available on Facebook is that of a brand: a business, an artist or musician, a nonprofit, a cause or a community. This persona collects fans, or as they are now known, "likes." The biggies, like Dunkin Donuts, Coke and Disney have tens of millions of fans. Some stars and celebrities choose to create a fan page rather than use their profile for fan interaction. The poster child for celebrity pages is Star Trek star George Takei, one of the most interesting and engaging people on Facebook, who has 4 million very interactive fans.

The biggest difference between a profile and a business page is that anyone can "like" a business page, but a profile has to approve connections before they can interact with the profile page.

Start relationships by being you, not just your business

If you've followed this book's arguments so far, you realize that creating relationships is one of the most powerful tools for building and growing a business. Personal profiles tend to be more relational than business pages. They offer fully two-way communication. You comment, like and post on other people's timelines and they will most likely do the same for you.

You connect with people a lot of ways outside of business. I am friends with people from grade school, high school and college; from my neighborhood, my town and my church. I've also made friends with people that I network with, teach, present to, and with my current and past clients. These people all interacting with tons of people on Facebook. I have gotten more than one inquiry from a person who asked Facebook friends, "Does anyone know somebody who can help me with Social Media?"

Create interactions by pictures and blog posts

Your sphere of influence goes way beyond work. Do you participate in golf or other sports as player or spectator, go to concerts or movies, have kids or pets, or enjoy wine, food, or anything else that people like to discuss, or learn about. Facebook connections are about person-to-person interests and interactions. Use those interests as springboards for text posts, photo shares and even video links.

You also can do things on Facebook as a person that you can't do as a business. One of the most important is to start and join groups. You can have open and closed groups. Groups can be used for homeowner associations, networking groups, alumni groups, secret groups, support groups and so on. These help build community in well-defined niches.

Finally, as yourself, you can like and interact with any Facebook page, personal or business. This means you can connect with more people, groups and information than if you only use a business page. If you feel comfortable doing so and it's appropriate, you can post on your business page, then share that post on your personal side as well. That can expand your reach since your personal friends (and their friends) may not be fans of your business. Also, if you are a nonprofit, band or someone who has events, once you've post events as a business and invited business likes and fans, you can also invite friends on the personal side as appropriate.

You can interact as yourself or your business

If you own a business, you should have a business page! Business pages let you connect with many more than the 5000-person profile friend limit. Depending on who you are, what your business does and whether you are regionally or nationally known, this may be essential for you. Also, Facebook's user agreement prohibits using a personal profile only as a business, so they will shut your page down if you do that and they find out.

What advantages do you get from using Facebook for your business?

- First off, it gives your brand a voice. If you are a business-to-consumer operation, it puts you in one of the most active and fluid forums. I have seen more than one company generate tons of business when they do Facebook right!

- Second, it can become an awesome customer support tool, but only if you are actively monitoring and fully utilizing it.

- Third, it's fun.

People come to Facebook for entertainment, not to be sold, so use your page with that in mind. I use what I call the 6, 9, 20 rule. If you post once a day, then you can post about your business on the seventh day and MAYBE offer something that sells your business. Post twice a day? Every tenth post can be about business. Three or more posts a day? Wait until your twenty-first post to do sales-related content. It's Not About You!

If you are posting funny pictures, great blogs or articles and stuff that interests your audience, you will get likes, comments and, most importantly, shares! If you are robo-posting (constantly selling or talking about yourself) you will see little or no interaction because people don't enjoy that. They want relationships and fun. Either you are a resource or you're noise! The best way to measure success for you, your competition and other businesses is to see how engaged people get on a page. Are they commenting, liking and sharing? If not, then something is not working!

Use your personal account to drive people to your business page. Let's say you've had an article printed on a local, regional, or national magazines website. You can then copy the link to that article onto your Facebook business page. Then share that post from your business page to your personal profile. That will alert all your friends as well as your fans—potentially thousands of people—that you produce, teach, present and write about your expertise. Talk about promoting a brand! How could something like that help promote YOUR brand, company, products or services?

Another advantage of a business page is that it lets you communicate with other businesses AS YOUR BUSINESS. When you change your posting persona to your business, you can start liking and commenting on other business pages. This can be a great way to interact with power partners and potential power partners. For instance, someone in the dog grooming business can like and trade comments with pooper scoopers, pet stores, dog walkers and veterinarians. You get the point—and your business name in front of all the people who like those businesses. Some may decide check you out also.

A word of caution: don't overdo it. People liked the other business first and most of them are savvy enough to smell (and block) a disingenuous marketer a mile away. Start off by genuinely helping other businesses promote themselves. Like and share their materials on your business timeline and you may find a kindred spirit (and with luck a few new customers).

Business pages offer analytics and multiple landing pages

Business pages also offer additional functionality that personal profiles don't.

These currently include

- importing blog posts

- additional landing pages

- collecting email addresses for your broadcast
  email systems

Most of that additional functionality comes through apps, those little programs that add flexibility and functionality to Facebook. Apps come in three flavors: free, paid-for and do–it-yourself. Yes, if you are geeky enough, you can make your own Facebook apps.

Some example of apps include those created by email programs like Constant Contact and IContact to allow you to collect email addresses for you newsletters by adding a tab, or RSS Graffiti, which lets your RSS feed from your blog auto-post to your business timeline. Paid options like Wildfire and others allow you to create contests, landing pages and more. All these options take Facebook for business to a whole new level.

A warning note about apps: Most apps are legit, but others are just a disguise for scammers. On the personal profile side, if the app gives the creator permission to post on your behalf, it can cause nasty problems. For instance, one night, my wife screamed at me to come quick. Her Facebook account had started posting pictures of 'Naked Rollerblading Women' Shortly after she'd liked an app on a friend's timeline purporting to support breast cancer. That app had grabbed permission to post on her timeline on her behalf. Tons of scams like that over the years have offered free airline tickets, IPhones, or IPads, or whatever the creators thought would get people to click, or like and add the app.

What they are looking for is your log-in information, so they can dig in deeper into your computer for banking and credit card information. Why 'Naked Rollerblading Women'? Porn attracts about as many people as 'European Lottery Winnings' emails! Scams and hackers come in many forms, so be careful who and what you trust! Needless to say, I removed the app and the problem went away!

Facebook now requires legit app developers to give you a choice of who can see what they post on your page (including just you) but still, use apps with caution!

Also, you have the control issue. I had used a free landing-page app for dozens of clients before, in the blink of an eye, it was shut down. I had to scramble and re-build multiple clients' landing pages in a new, trusted and paid-for app. So be careful and aware when adding apps on the personal or business side of your Facebook account.

You can find thousands of books, blogs and articles on the mechanics of how to make Facebook work for your business. Unfortunately, some are outdated before they are printed because it all changes so fast. But buy a few, read some online and give their techniques a shot.

The best advice I can offer you is to dive in. Once you've started, look at the big boys and your competition to see what they are doing and what's working. Then try something and measure results. Keep doing what works and stop doing what doesn't!

If you sell to consumers, you can't afford to ignore how many people use Facebook to recommend businesses that they KNOW, LIKE and TRUST!

CHAPTER 20: LINKEDIN

BACON-IZMS

- LinkedIn is all about business-to-business

- Build a personal profile for peer–to-peer connections

- Put together a good, professional profile

- Get recommendations and testimonials

- Connect with people through groups

- Connect your business to anyone in the world

- Paid-for Premium - is it worth the $$?

LinkedIn is all about business and about all businesses. Both business-to–consumer (B2C) and business-to-business (B2B) are welcome here. It's growing at a rapid pace, in part because of the recognition that this social networking space focuses on connecting business people with business people.

Also, the down economy has driven many more people to LinkedIn for job searches, to post their resumes and to form and use connections to get a leg up on competition.

LinkedIn is all about business-to-business

Unlike Facebook, which wants your profile to list your favorite movies, music, sports teams and personal stuff, LinkedIn is ALL business. It combines a resume, a CV (curriculum vitae) and networking platform in one package. It also allows you to share news, articles, blogs and more with connections.

Build a personal profile for peer-to-peer connections

The LinkedIn experience begins with how you present yourself. Some people think of the resume classes they took years ago, while others think you should use a big sales pitch. Neither is true. LinkedIn is really about two things, clarity and keywords.

One of the biggest functional differences between Facebook and LinkedIn is that LinkedIn has an excellent built-in search engine. If you build a good profile, chances are that a search for yourself in Google, will show your LinkedIn profile at the top of the search.

Put together a good, professional profile

Start with a current, professional headshot. Yes, you can take a picture with your phone camera or use a shot from your vacation photos, but I don't recommend it. A good-quality headshot is an investment, not an expense. Also, make it a current photo. You may have looked better 10 or 20 years ago, but you want to be recognized now. When I meet face-to-face with someone for the first time, I normally go to the LinkedIn profile to see a current picture of what the person looks like.

How do you get that killer profile picture? Find someone you network with whose profile picture blows you away and ask them who took it. An investment of $50 to $250 could make the difference between getting and missing out on business.

Next, optimize the effectiveness of your professional headline. Why is this so important? If someone searches for you, this headline could make your first impression. Most people just use their business title, "Director of Sales and Marketing at XYZ Company." Even worse: "In Transition."

Try to do something creative, expressive and dynamic. My current headline reads "Nationally Recognized Author, Strategist & Speaker on Social Media, Internet Marketing & Google". You could change "Sales Manager" to "Leading Expert on Manufacturing Processes and Successful Digital Integration for the Food Industry". I'm not telling you to exaggerate or distort what you really do, just find a more descriptive or engaging way to say it.

Then look at your summary, where you give people the detailed insight to all that you do and have done, what makes you unique. Keywords work for you in this section. Include any applicable key search terms from your field or industry. Don't keyword it to death, though, because people will be reading and you need them to understand what you do and what you have to offer them.

Another point to consider is how you write your summary. If you write in the first person, all those I's and We's can sound a bit self-serving. Make you profile summary more readable by writing it in the third person. You may find this hard at first, but third person makes your summary read more like a bio from a business website. If writing isn't your strength, consider hiring a writer to help organize your content into a strong, professional-sounding summary.

Get recommendations and testimonials

The third, and most important, part of a LinkedIn profile is the recommendations. Don't confuse recommendations with endorsements. Recommendations are personal, written testimonials about your work and your skills. Endorsements, a relatively new feature that LinkedIn added to try to increase activity, mostly serve to remind inactive members that LinkedIn is still there.

When you sign in, LinkedIn now shows you an influencer and says, "Your connections A and B, and 18 others have endorsed you for new skills and expertise". That baits you into returning the favor. If you want to, you can endorse people for 'Basket Weaving' or 'Nuclear Science' (skills that have nothing to do with them or their jobs). So, endorsements are a nice gesture, but may have little credibility with connections.

Recommendations, on the other hand, relate personal experiences of people that verified work connections with you. Recommendations carry weight and credibility. You get recommendations by asking contacts for them. If they agree, they must actively confirm that you have worked together in some fashion and write a testimonial in their own words. By the way, you get to approve each, with the option not to display an indiscreet recommendation.

If you ask for recommendations, people expect you to return the favor. You can prime the pump by starting the process. Just write a recommendation for someone you respect. Many will return the favor without you having to ask. (LinkedIn even prompts them to do so.)

Recommendations are another form of testimonials. They form a foundation for TRUST. So just using LinkedIn to garner recommendations will earn a bonus for your business.

Connect with people through groups

Next, work on getting connections. Give your complete job history, starting with your current position and filling in as much detail as possible. Then add each of your past jobs in reverse order of dates you started and ended. In the classes I've taught to people looking for jobs, some hesitate to include jobs where they were let go. Why? Someone else who left or was let go from the same firm may now work at a company you'd like to join. That person could become a million dollar connection. When I added Arthur Andersen to my profile, I immediately got the opportunity to connect with 70,000+ people worldwide, and I've connected with many of them.

Another way to find connections is to let LinkedIn search your email contact lists for those already on LinkedIn. From time to time, LinkedIn will also suggest additional connections based on connections you already have. People may reach out to connect with you from receiving their own suggested new connections.

Some people only connect with people who they actually know, while others connect with everybody who asks. But beyond direct connections, whenever you join groups, you connected the group's members, potentially thousands of people you may or may not know. You have to figure out who will bring a good alliance and who will just be an annoyance. I tend to limit my connections to only people in the US except for people I have met face to face.

You can also use LinkedIn to research potential connections for a leg in the door, either as a vendor or potential employee. Search for the company in which you're interested. Do any of your first-level connections (people with whom you have already connected) work there? If not, maybe you have a second-level connection, someone at the company who's connected to someone you already know. To follow up, click on the second-level connection at the company to see which of your connections know the company contact. If you know that connection well enough, you can ask for an introduction. You may be able to turn a second level connection into a first-level, to whom you can send messages and with whom you may build a relationship. I have also seen people use this technique to get their resume to the top of the pile during a job search.

Connect with people through groups

Joining groups is a power-user technique. LinkedIn currently has more than 1.5 million groups, which can be open or private. They can be for business or hobbies. You can join groups for Guitar Players or Musicians, Mac or PC Enthusiasts, Industry Groups or Think Tanks and Networking or Support groups. I belong to all of those plus my local Chamber of Commerce groups. I have started and currently manage a few LinkedIn groups for local networking groups I belong to.

You can belong to up to 50 groups at a time. You can also control how much your groups inform and interact with you. You can choose daily or weekly digests of group activities, or request no emails from specified groups.

So, what can you do with groups? That depends on the type of group.

• Some groups are great for getting and giving help. Post questions and you can get answers to technical or business problems.

- Other groups are great for networking. You can get to know people better and even make connections for your or other businesses.

- Some are great for learning.

LinkedIn has tons of groups; your industry will have at least a few, places where people post the latest news, blogs, questions and opinions. Other group members then like, comment and interact with posts.

Speaking of posts, groups can be a great way to increase discussion of your blog. Post a link to a specific post so people can click through to read it on your website. Most will probably like or comment. Even posting links to someone else's interesting blog or article is a good way to start conversations.

What should you not do? Don't over-sell or over-post. I have seen people kill groups by posting ad after ad after ad, asking people to come to their events or selling their products. If one member dominates group conversations with ads, others will ignore or leave the group. Each group's manager should control how people use the group and act to stop abuse. The best groups have an active membership with people who speak up and stop spammers.

Connect your business to everyone in the world

LinkedIn also allows you to create a page for your business. If you have employees, this allows them to become social advocates and grow the sphere of influence of your business. Even for a solopreneur, a business can still bring advantages. On LinkedIn, as on Facebook, individuals must search out and like or follow your business. Any posting you do as your business shows up in your followers' news feeds.

If you need good information, you can follow industry magazines or competitive companies. Because some businesses post much more than others on their pages, look for the ones with the most, and most useful, posts.

Paid-for Premium, is it worth the $$?

LinkedIn Premium, a monthly subscription upgrade, offers several advantages. The upgrade lets you can contact second- and third-level contacts directly by InMail. It also lets you see everyone who has viewed your profile and their profiles. And it has advanced search and introduction capabilities. However, Premium can cost you hundreds to thousands of dollars a year. Unless you are a power sales person, these pluses may not give you enough benefit beyond what the free version offers to be worth the added cost.

Like all social networking tools, LinkedIn's features change frequently. LinkedIn offers far more capabilities and tools than I have time to mention in this book, but I can tell you that it's one of the best business networking tools out there. Even if you use it only to get to know more about people you network with, it's invaluable.

CHAPTER 21:
TWITTER

BACON-IZMS

Twitter sends 140-character max text messages

- Use Twitter for broadcast messages or personal messaging

- As with TV and radio, dial in to get what you want

- Narrow Twitter feeds with searches and hashtags

- Web address shortening sites make long URLs usable

- Keep Tweets under 120 characters to promote re-tweeting

Twitter is one of the most popular, most underutilized and least understood of the social networks. Every class or presentation I give, I ask two questions:

"Who is on Twitter?" A bunch, usually around half the group, raise their hands.

"Who understands Twitter?" Usually only one or two hands stay up.

I hope this chapter will give you a better understanding of what Twitter is and what it can do for you and your business.

Twitter sends 140-character max text messages

Twitter in its purest form is a micro blog limited to 140 characters. It was originally designed as an SMS (short message service), usually associated with text messages sent on cell phones. SMS was originally peer-to-peer or person-to-person. Twitter allows you to broadcast your message to a group of people.

Twitter launched in 2006 and has gained more than 500 million users. You don't have to follow anyone or register with Twitter to read tweets. It's kind of a Wild West compared to other social networks. And once you register, you get the chance to communicate with other Twitter members, directly or indirectly.

Two aspects of Twitter drive people crazy: "What can I possibly say or do with only 140 characters?" and "As fast as I can refresh, all the twitter posts are gone!" Guess what, they're not gone, just replaced by new ones. The day Michael Jackson died, Twitter received more than 1,000 tweets per second. No one can read that fast, so how can you possibly keep up with it?

Use Twitter for broadcast messages OR personal messaging

People use Twitter in one of two ways: as a text messaging service to communicate with individuals or groups or as an informational tool that can both broadcast and receive messages.

People use Twitter to communicate with family, friends and followers using codes like DM (direct message) and

@ (mention) to keep everyone in their community in the loop. This can work fine if your family and friends are Twitter savvy. But that's a topic for another book.

The second way people use Twitter is as a news, story, blog and technical-support aggregator. People in places like Egypt and now Syria have used Twitter and other social network tools to circumvent government restrictions and report on (and coordinate) uprising events on.

Most news agencies now get information and report news on Twitter first. Granted, it's not always accurate, but it's fast and very active. Tons of articles that start out on blogs and news sites get shared on Twitter. With so much information happening so fast, people can't keep up with it. At least the ones who don't learn how to use the tool.

As with TV and radio, dial in to get what you want

The best way I can explain Twitter to newbies (and sometimes avid users) is this: In the days before HDTV and remotes, people used rabbit-ear antennas and tin foil to improve reception. You not only had to get up to change the channel, but you had to use a fine-tune dial to get the clearest picture.

Even today, you have multiple channels of TV signals floating through the sky. The TV actually received all those signals; the tuner allowed you to dial in one channel at a time, whether VHF (very high frequency) or UHF (very high frequency), depending on what you wanted to watch. At the same time, radio stations broadcast AM or FM signals on dozens of other frequencies, and you needed another device (called a radio) to receive and serve up the music or talk.

Think of Twitter as the equivalent of all those UHF, VHF, AM, FM and other signals: messages just floating across the internet. It's your job to dial it in.

What you generally see (depending on the number of people you follow) is all of those signals, unscrambled and unfiltered. It's just a lot of noise until you start to tune into certain channels.

Narrow Twitter feeds by searches and hashtags

You can use lots of techniques to tune in and filter out content, both inside and outside of Twitter. Let's start with inside Twitter.

Twitter does some filtering for you with 'Trending Topics,' a feed that tracks what lots of people are talking about. When a big news story trends (lots of people tweeting about it), it jumps to the top of the list. Twitter says, "Trends offer a unique way to get closer to what you care about. They are tailored for you based on your location and who you follow."

Another way to channel is to search. Simply go to the search bar and type what you are looking for. Twitter will narrow down what you see by that topic.

Akin to search is the hashtag or # sign. Twitter uses hashtags to group content in ways that make a subject or discussion easier to follow. Search #Bacon and you will see posts where people included that hashtag in their tweet. The hashtag does not care about upper- or lower-case, but spelling counts.

A common use of hashtags is by groups or trade shows like #NABShow or #CHA2013. People add this hashtag to tweets to help others find content for specific events.

Hashtags are also used for something called Tweet Chats. These are weekly open forums that happen at specific times. I have attended #blogchat on Sunday nights from 8-9pm Central time. Depending on how many people attend, it can present a mind meld of topics and conversations about blogging. Dozens of tweet chats every day cover a wide range of personal and business topics. To learn more, Google "Tweet Chats."

A good tool for that is tweetchat.com, where you can log in with your Twitter account and enter a tweet chat name, such as #blogchat. The service not only filters content but also adds the hashtag for you in each tweet and reply.

A great tool for both narrowing down content and attending tweet chats is HootSuite. HootSuite is a free (or paid–for, your choice) web-based tool, that works with most social networks, but is particularly useful with Twitter. It shows you your tweets, mentions and direct messages. It also allows you to create search streams or columns. You can have multiple streams in multiple columns and monitor specific topics that interest you. That makes Hootsuite a perfect tool for attending and monitoring tweet chats or following other content.

Web address shortening sites make long URLs usable

You can also use Twitter to share your blogs and articles. Unfortunately, most of the time the URL you want to share has much more than 140 characters, so how can that work?

Twitter will shorten the link for you and maintain the integrity of the URL, but it's better if you take control that yourself, by using a URL shortener service like TinyURL.com, goo.gl, or Bit.ly. They all take any size URL and reduce it to

20-30 characters. Bit.ly will let you create an account that gives you analytics on clicks and shares.

Goo.gl does a similar job and will keep track for you using your gmail login.

Keep Tweets under 120 characters to promote re-tweeting

With only 140 characters to a tweet, you need to know some best practices to follow. First off, it's best not to use all 140 characters. Try to use 120 at most. This allows room for someone to re-tweet your message with a mention or add their own hashtag of choice.

The best tweets (and the most re-tweeted ones), start with a compelling headline or call to action (60-80 characters), followed by the shortened URL (20-30 characters). You can end by adding a hashtag or two (your remaining 10-50 characters). The goal is to get as much attention and network traction as possible.

You can set some social networks to automatically tweet for you from their interface. You can simul-post from Facebook to Twitter, or LinkedIn to Twitter, but they don't give you the format just outlined above. And if you add hashtags to Facebook or LinkedIn posts, not everyone will get it. Some even may look at #usinghashtags as being #toospammy in spaces other than Twitter.

You will get your best results by not linking social network accounts. You can accomplish a similar result using a tool like HootSuite to post directly to Twitter.

Are you beginning to see how you can use Twitter? And not only how to organize the chaos, but how to help your business with it? Well, that how does depend on your business.

I have a client who owns a wine store in Geneva, IL. (Check out GibbysWine.com.) The store learned how to use Twitter to find people who talk about #wine. Maybe those people said "Today's #wine line up, 2011 Villa Creek Pink & 2007 Carlisle Zinfandel Carlisle Vineyard." I suggested that Gibby's should follow people who talk about wines and not necessarily wineries, distributors or other wine stores, because when you follow someone, they will often follow you back.

Now, every time new posts appear in the store's blog, they share it on Twitter. It's a great way to inform followers about new wines that have come in or report on their annual trips to Napa and Sonoma Valley to visit the wineries.

I have seen businesses monitor Twitter for tweets from potential customers who are sharing their dislike for a competitor's product or service, so they can direct message unsatisfied customers with an offer or a coupon to lure them away from the competitor. Someone who was unhappy with service on their motorcycle, for instance, might get an offer for a free oil change along with a 10-point safety inspection.

A takeout business like a coffee shop can allow customers to tweet in orders, so the shop can give them curb side service even though the shop does not have a drive-thru lane. That way, patrons get great customer service without having to search for a parking spot or taking the time to park and walk in!

Large corporations monitor both unhappy and happy tweets so they can respond to them. When someone posts a negative about a hotel, a store, or an internet service, a customer service rep messages back, trying to make the bad experience better. When someone tweets a compliment, they may @message them back, thanking the person who sent in the message and letting all their followers read about the positive experience.

Twitter can often be more about what other are posting than what you post... It's Not About You!

Your business can use Twitter many ways. You can use it as another distribution tool for your blog posts and for articles you write or are mentioned in. It's a great way to share your content that's also a great way to connect with and learn from others.

I have to admit Twitter can be an acquired taste because it's not as visual and interactive as Facebook or LinkedIn, although some might argue that it's more inter-active. Nonetheless, it's one of the greatest interactive sources of news and information on the internet.

CHAPTER 22: PINTEREST

BACON-IZMS

- Pinterest offers a virtual pin board

- Multiple pin boards handle your multiple interests

- Pin your own material or re-pin from others

- People can follow you and you can follow others

- Be careful about copyright when pinning

- You can have both personal and business accounts

- Pins can link back to your website or blog

Pinterest (Pin+interest) is the new kid on the block. By far the most visual social networking tool, it has driven Facebook, LinkedIn and others to more graphic and image-friendly functionality!

Pinterest offers a virtual pin board

Pinterest uses the metaphor that it's a pin board for ideas and items you want to collect and save for later reference. It's perfect for helping you plan your wedding, save recipes, collect hobby and craft ideas or whatever you want. People started sharing art, fashion, tech, nostalgia and much more.

Pinterest's core concept is simple yet effective. You create an account and get a blank slate with only two main components: boards and pins.

You may remember the old cork boards or the fabric walls of your corporate cubical. You would take a note from a notepad, grab a pushpin and pin the note to the board for visible future reference. While papers in your in box sat, getting buried, those notes stayed in plain view.

Multiple pin boards handle your multiple interests

You can create as many Pinterest pin boards as you want. That helps you segment topics you want to keep track of. You choose the topics and how you want to compartmentalize them, perhaps recipes, home repair and fashion. Or art, soccer and fishing. In the case of your business, you might choose infographics, webpages, marketing tips, or whatever you want to collect.

Pin your own material or re-pin from others

You also can use two kinds of pins: text or pictorial items you create and pin to your boards, or pins you find else-where and re-pin to your own boards. You can choose to "like" others' pins as well as re-pin them for your reference. Reciprocally, people who find your boards and pins can re-pin both your original pins and those you've re-pinned from others. It's easy to see how one pin can end up on dozens or hundreds of boards and get Pinterest virality.

People can follow you and you can follow others

You can choose to follow other users and have access to all their boards, or you may choose to simply like or re-pin a post. That re-pin maintains a link to the original post, so the originator of the pin maintains credit for the post. You can also see all the people you follow and have access to all their boards and pins. Your account will show your followers and pins from you that have been re-pinned.

Following people gives you the benefit of being able to organize people whose content you like within your own account. The same goes for people who follow you.

Be careful about copyright when pinning

You can find content to pin both inside and outside of Pinterest. The simplest and most obvious is logging into Pinterest and using the search feature. Search for a word like 'Bacon' to find literally thousands of posts ranging from pictures to jokes to recipes to pictures of Kevin Bacon made out of Bacon. Search for "Bacon Recipes" to narrow the scope of your search. Find something you like? Just re-pin it to one of your boards. But especially when you are pinning to extend your brand, keep in mind those others who can see and share what you pin... It's Not About You.

Another way is to add your own pins. You can either pin a file that you upload from your computer, or you can use a URL from either your website or anothers'. Once you've added the content, you get to choose which existing board to pin to, or you can create a new board for it.

A word of caution. If you have not yet read chapter 17 on creative rights, do so right now. A lot of buzz has hit the internet about how the user agreement you sign when you create a Pinterest account protects THEM, but does not totally indemnify YOU when posting copyrighted materials. The scary part is, this means that if you re-pin content that someone else originally pinned without noting that it's copyrighted, you may not be protected if the copyright owner chooses to pursue a complaint.

It has yet to become a problem since most content is considered commentary and thus covered by fair use , but if the owner can make a plausible case that it's being used for business, your pin could become an issue.

You can have both personal and business accounts

Pinterest recently added Pinterest for Business. The biggest difference between a personal and a business account is the addition of analytics, allowing you to see how people are viewing and re-pinning your content.

If you use Pinterest as your business, you're expanding your brand. You get to add your business information in your profile, plus you can keep your personal pins personal and your business pins strictly business.

Another thing that you can do on either business or personal accounts is create 'Secret Boards,' that only you can see. That means you can use Pinterest as a marketing tool, but also as it was originally intended: as a place to organize and keep ideas for your own business.

Pins can link back to your website or blog

So how do businesses benefit by using Pinterest? Well, in a couple of ways.

The first is the most obvious. If you have products or deliverables, surely having pictures of those being liked, commented on and re-pinned could help your business.

Also, having people share your content is one of the best ways to grow your brand. With a well-thought-out Pinterest board can get your business in front of a bunch of people who don't know about you and may be interested in your products and or services.

The second and maybe the most powerful benefit comes when the URL for your graphics gets shared.

For example, when I write my blog, I share images from it to my Pinterest account. I hope that people share and re-pin the image, but what I really hope is that they also click on the image. If they do, then my blog post opens in a new window, sharing my blog and my website with the user. And yes, that can be tracked with Google Analytics so I can see how much traffic is being generated from my Pinterest account.

If you operate in any of the craft, food, fashion, or creative industries, you should try connecting with others through Pinterest. Use it to share your ideas and content. The better, more creative and interesting the images you pin, the better chance you have of creating a buzz about your business on Pinterest.

CHAPTER 23: GOOGLE+

BACON-IZMS

- Google+ is Google's answer to Facebook

- You can have a personal account and a business page

- Marketing your business on Google

- Circles can segment friends and acquaintances

- Communities mimic LinkedIn, Facebook groups

- Make video chat hangouts open or closed

Google+ is Google's answer to Facebook

Google+ is Google's attempt to compete with Facebook in the social networking arena. Most people have a hard enough time keeping up with one social network, but this newcomer can be an important tool in certain situations.

First off, if you have a gmail account, you have Google+ already attached to it. If and how you use it is up to you.

Just as with Facebook and LinkedIn, you have the options of a personal and business presence, through a Google+ profile and a Google+ business page.

Google does not use the friends or connections metaphor. It uses Circles. This allows you to group your connections as to how, when and why you want to communicate with them. I have circles for my friends, my family, business, news, sports, church, and so on. Then Google+ lets you filter to see updates from just selected people in each of your circles. It helps cut down the noise and lets you focus each circle individually.

You can have a personal account and a business page

Google+ business pages offer one of the most powerful and useful tools for most business users. You can easily create one from your Google+ account and also add multiple pages. So, if you've written multiple books, you can have a separate page for each book. If you have a business with multiple locations, you can (and should) create a page for each location.

Just as on other social networks, you can switch personas and post as either your business or yourself. You can also add people to your business's circles, separate from your personal circles. Businesses can do hangouts and join communities as well, but remember what I said earlier about operating P2P, not just B2B.

A few things make Google+ a must-have if you operate a local brick–and-mortar store and use Google to promote online. Most importantly, Google+ business pages integrate into Google Maps and Google Places. If you are in Google+, you show up in the local tab. The information you post on your Google+ business page gets used across other Google properties. The good news is: less entering the same data in multiple places. The problem is: navigating the matrix of what feeds what, which changes all the time.

At a minimum, it's a good idea to claim and complete your Google+ business page profile. Google boasts 500+ million users and 250+ million active users. Google+ tends to have more a technical or geeky audience but it's slowly moving toward the mainstream.

Marketing your business on Google

Let's look at the basics of Google+ and its capabilities for your networking and your business.

Your profile: Your profile is tied to your Google Accounts, so you set it up as part of your overall Google account. If you have already set up a gmail account, you don't have to start all over. You can add a profile picture, a cover photo and details about you and where you work, just like in most other social media accounts. Obviously, the more complete you make the profile, the more likely the right people will find you and connect.

Interaction: To connect with people on Google+, you can go to their profile and share something or comment on their posts. You can mention them in your posts by adding a +[their-name]. You can start a hangout (video chat, covered later in this chapter).

Unlike Facebook, you don't "like" posts, you give a "+1" to posts. But just like in other social networks, you can comment on posts, so the goal of creating interaction stays pretty much the same.

Circles can segment your friends and acquaintances

As in most other social networks, once you've added someone to your circles, you can see who he or she has in his or her circles and add the friends-of-friends to your circles, too. Unlike with LinkedIn and Facebook, connections don't have to accept or approve being added to your circle. That makes it easier to connect but, in some people's minds, diminishes the value of circles.

You can also simply look people up via search. Some of the most popular or techie celebrities (like Andy Ihnatko and Guy Kawasaki) and celebrities like Lady Gaga and Richard Branson use Google+. As does the Dalai Lama.

As mentioned before, circles are easy to set up for easy filtering of posts by type or topic.

Communities mimic LinkedIn, Facebook groups

Communities in Google+ work much like groups in Facebook or LinkedIn. They can be closed or open, and a Google+ member starts and moderates them. One of the biggest differences being able to create categories for discussion topics. This helps members focus on what they consider most. Like groups in other networks, a lot of good information gets posted in communities including links to articles and blogs.

Choose open or closed video chat hangouts

Google Hangouts are essentially video chatrooms or conference calls. In most cases, to start a hangout you will need to install a Google voice and video plug-in. Hangouts, scheduled or impromptu, can be started and ended at any time.

I have some friends who swear by them. Myself, I have a face for radio and, although I have cameras on every computer and phone I own, I am not inclined to use them for social networking. With that said, It's Not About You, (or me)... it's about your audience.

Just to name a few possible uses, hangouts can function as virtual meetings, networking groups, think tanks or customer support. As long as the people you want to communicate with actively use Google+, you can harness a lot of potential with this format.

Even if you are sure you don't have time for ANOTHER social network, you owe it to yourself and your business to at least claim your Google+ account and business page. Fill out your profiles as completely as possible and check back every once in a while to see what's happening there.

Since Google is such a huge player on the internet, it's not going away soon. Also, the integration of Google+ with Maps, Places, Analytics, Adwords, Calendar and more can make this a powerful and useful tool to help you build and enhance your network.

If you are in the technology sector, then this is a no-brainer. You have to get in and join in on the communities, hangouts and conversations that are happening.

It's also a great way to share your content and connect up with a diverse community of people.

CHAPTER 24:
YOUTUBE/VIMEO

BACON-IZMS

- Video is powerful because it's visual and auditory

- YouTube ranks #2 in internet searches behind #1 Google

- Video quality represents the quality of your product/service

- Quality matters less in training or face-to-face videos

- PowerPoints can become killer internet marketing tools

- Vimeo can protect your videos from being shared

Video is a power tool when it comes to web marketing. It's one of the most powerful tools you can use with internet marketing but to get it at its artistic best, you need a professional. That does not mean you can't do a good do-it-yourself video, but know when and where quality counts.

Video is powerful because it's visual and auditory

Why do TV commercials cost hundreds of times more to produce and broadcast than radio commercials? Because they are much more complicated to produce and much more powerful when done right.

Video combines visual impact with voice and music to create very emotional and powerful ways of communicating. Don't get me wrong, radio as theater of the mind can be totally successful and powerful, but visuals add another dimension to your messages.

Soundtracks can make or break a movie. Just watch something like Star Wars without the sound. Where did the dramatic tension go? Listen to the sound with the screen black and you may not be able to follow the complete story.

YouTube ranks #2 in internet searches behind #1 Google

Google's search capabilities account for 80% of all internet search traffic. What is the number two search engine? It's not Yahoo or Bing, It's YouTube (which Google now owns). More than 100,000 videos get uploaded every day! Luckily, you are not competing against the world, just your competition! Vimeo is a good YouTube alternative, for reasons I will discuss at the end of this chapter.

If you produce a video, you can upload it to YouTube. If you set it up with the right title, good keywords in the description and the right permissions, it can and will be shared and has the potential to go viral. I'm sure you've seen dozens of viral dog, cat and kid videos. If you can produce something that people want to watch and share, it has a good chance of going beyond your own YouTube channel.

If you have a gmail account, you already have access to YouTube by signing in at YouTube.com with your gmail account. Otherwise, just create a gmail account. Once you sign in, you can create your own YouTube Channel, where all the videos you upload are associated with your account.

So, you have some videos to share with the world. Once they are uploaded and processed, you can view and share them on all your social media and websites.

You can share by a simple URL link, which starts with http://www.youtube.com/ followed by the data that links to your video. Right below your video, you will find a share button and the full share URL. Or you can find it in your browser's URL at the top of the window. Just copy and paste the URL in an email or a post on Facebook, Google+, or other social media to share the video with the world.

You can also share using the embed code. This writes iframe or html code and lets you embed the video in your blog or website. It even lets you choose quality and size. While using embeds takes a little more knowledge and patience, it gives you much more control over how your video is viewed.

Either way, YouTube will let you know how any times your video has been viewed and in most cases will allow others to share it, increasing the ability for it to go viral.

Embedded video will increase time people spend on your website (at least long enough to watch the video). Sharing, increases the number of views. So you have a much better opportunity to connect and reach a larger audience.

Video quality represents the quality of your product/service

Good quality video starts with good equipment and good software. Professional cameras (not the ones you get at Best Buy) can run between $3000 and $30,000, or more. Most video editors use either Final Cut Pro, Adobe Premier, or professional systems like AVID and others. Some "lite" versions of these can be bought for around $100 but most cost more. Tack on mics, audio gear, headphones, lighting equipment at a minimum, and you've accumulated some big expense.

Then you have to make the time to learn how to operate all the equipment and software. You'll need a computer and hard drive storage that can handle working with all this gear and the mammoth video files. Sometime it just makes more sense to hire a pro.

If you look, you will no doubt find some very good and experienced video producers and crews in your area. Networking is a good source for meeting or hearing about them. Depending on the scope of your video, it can cost much less to hire it done than to buy the equipment you'd need.

Back when I worked at AT&T, I was told one day that today was the day I would become a cameraman. I was totally excited until I learned that the camera I was holding on my shoulder was worth twice as much as my house (yep, the Ikegami HL-79 camera, same quality as cameras used on the nightly news at the time, was worth $79,000 and my townhouse was worth a mere $38,000). Needless to say, that first time I shot video, it was a little shaky, but over time I got much better!

Fast forward to today. Most cell phones, IPads, laptops have high resolution cameras and software that enhances and stabilizes video (most of them HD: High Definition).

Even my car has a camera in its bumper (and soon it will be Bluetooth recordable).

Nothing says you need feature film quality production for your online video, but you shouldn't produce garbage either! It's Not About You.

I have read about and listened to more than one video or webinar that said creating video online is the key to success. OK. But I've seen people run with the idea and do more harm than good! In the world of 3D, HDTV and BluRay disc, quality counts.

Cautionary tale: I was asked to get involved in a company a few years ago. It was a startup that was going to be the next Avon, Tupperware or whichever wildly successful multilevel marketer you care to mention. I agreed to look at the website and was later recruited to participate in the marketing.

I watched the online videos. Their quality was less than stellar and the audio changed from segment to segment and clip to clip. You heard the CEO talking about how if you joined in on the startup level, you would get rich beyond your wildest dreams. The camera was 10 feet away and the CEO had no mic, so you heard the boom of the room but the CEO sounded muffled and echo-y!

My experience and gut told me that, if they did not put quality in at this level, they never would, and the company didn't last six months.

Most computers use external speakers with incredible quality. Mine has a Bose system with a subwoofer, so I can hear whether your sound quality is excellent, passable or not even. Internet users pay much more attention to these details than some people give them credit for. The quality of the audio and video reflects a lot about the quality of your product or service.

Success Story: I have a client who sells hardware and software for septage receiving stations, where Porta-Potty and other waste disposal trucks go to empty their loads. He wanted to produce a video aimed at the workers in the four main functional areas of his business: the operations manager who works with the staff and trucks, the office staff who handle paperwork and billing, the IT department that deals with hardware and software operation and integration, and the truck drivers who have to manage their own manifests and paperwork.

We hired a professional narrator to read the client's script. While only a 5-minute piece, it needed to address all four audiences. Once we'd finished with music and editing, it really only felt like a 3-minute video. We uploaded it to YouTube and also posted it on the website for that product.

A short time later, it started showing up in searches on Google for 'Septage Receiving Station.' The business was getting calls and emails from all over the world, expanding their reach well beyond anything that a sales team locally could do. It only took one sale to more than recoup the cost of the professional production and it's still producing results years later.

Quality matters less in training or face-to-face videos

Not every video on the internet needs award-winning production values. If you have ever seen or been involved in a Skype meeting, sometimes that can be enough to engage and convince people that you and your products or services are the right choice for them. As a matter of fact, Skype or other web meetings and webinars can be incredible powerful and successful for marketing products. It really depends on your audience and their expectations.

Key factors for video that works are light on the subjects and good audio quality. Positioning a person or subject so the light or sun shines on their face and using an external microphone or lapel mic can do wonders to improve quality. I have a USB mic on my desk that I use to produce my how-to videos. The quality is outstanding, but even seeing a headset on a subject is acceptable and better than using the built-in mic on a laptop.

PowerPoints can become killer internet marketing tools

One way to produce killer video on a budget is something I call PowerPoint on Steroids: an online presentation that has the elements of a professional video without the filming expense:

- Well-planned content

- Good quality graphics

- A well-written script

- Good narration

- Well-chosen background music

How does it work? First, you assemble your presentation in Powerpoint, Keynote, or your favorite presentation software. Then, record yourself or a professional narrator reading your script. Edit out the mistakes and re-takes.

Next, use a screen capture software like Camtasia, Jing (PC or Mac) or ScreenFlow (Mac only). You play the audio and advance the presentation while the screen capture software records both audio and visuals. These programs let you edit later, adding transitions and special effect— just don't overdo the post production. For the finishing, polished touch, you can import a music track for the opening and closing credits or throughout the entire project.

Once you finish the editing, some programs allow you to upload directly into your YouTube or Vimeo accounts.

A couple of additional thoughts about creating these videos. There is no lower limit on how short they can be, but they can be too long. Two or three minutes (the length of the average pop song) is as much as most people will watch to the end let alone retain most of the information.

Also, YouTube does set limits on how long a video can be when uploaded on their free accounts. Sometimes you have to go longer, as with a 1/2 hour or hour-long webinar, for instance. Other times it makes sense to cut longer videos into smaller, more digestible pieces.

Vimeo can protect your videos from being shared

Vimeo is a good free and paid for alternative to YouTube. It does not have video length limits, but does, like YouTube limit file size. It also offers a bit more control over your video than YouTube. This is especially useful if you want to make your videos private within their software, so you can display them on a subscription-only web site.

If you are trying to make your video go viral, then YouTube may be the better choice. If you want more control in how your videos are shared and need to protect content, then Vimeo may suit your needs better.

Having been a videographer, editor and producer, I look at online video with more of a critical eye. Then again, I understand how powerful good video can be for your business. Even a simple video that I made of my dog fetching a ball worked as a great networking tool on Facebook. I made it by putting my IPad on the grass and throwing the ball for him.

I did the same thing to produce promo videos for my band, Doughboyz.com. The quality of my IPad audio and video were sufficient for the need of the message and audience expectations. Sometimes simple is all you need.

Be sure to consider your brand and your audience when producing and sharing video online. No matter what you use to produce your video and how you share it, video can be one of the most powerful communication tools in your networking arsenal!

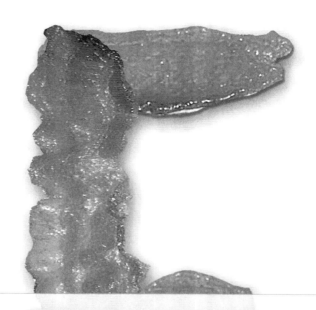

PART 5: BRING IT HOME

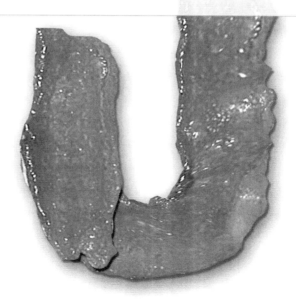

The new methodologies available on the internet have changed how we build relationships. So far in this book, you've learned how and why people get to KNOW, LIKE and TRUST you. We've explored why you need a website, measurement tools and traffic generation to build a solid relational network. Then we covered how to define and build audiences and the tools of the trade we use to communicate, to nurture and grow relationships.

You've learned that it's not enough to be actively networking and social networking. You have to become a trusted resource that people actively search for and reach out to. By creating and sharing awesome content, you will stand above the crowd of competition and have a much better chance of going viral.

In this last section, we will examine the power of great content, how to distribute it and how to create intentional interaction and engagement. Using all that, we will explore how to create a memorable brand that will help you rise above the noise and stay relevant to your networks.

CHAPTER 25:
CONTENT IS KING

BACON-IZMS

- Content creates connections

- Don't just robo-post

- Write original content to become a thought leader

- Email marketing should drive people to your website

- Blogs can be a great way to share content

- White papers and ebooks share your ideas
  and knowledge

- Produce content that people want to share

I talked about knowing your audience in Chapter 15. You have to know who you are talking TO before you can talk WITH them and not just AT them. Before you can create conversations, you have to know what they want to talk about. What interests them? What excites them? What brings out passions or stirs up the pot? It's up to you to be the catalyst for conversations. It's Not About You... it's about your audience!

Just being on social networking and commenting on cat pictures will not get you anywhere unless you work in the pet industry and/or want to adopt lots of cats. You need to be interactive to create and build relationships. You have to feed your page, if you want people to read your page, but you also have to comment and interact to promote interaction. You can't be just a consumer, you have to jump in and be a source of goodness.

Content creates connections

Good content is in the eye of the beholder. Sometimes and for some audiences, it's new information about tools or techniques, while at other times and places, it might be a new spin or controversial perspective on a popular concept. Either way, you have to be enlightening and entertaining and enhance what they may or may not already know. The key here is to be a KNOWN, LIKED and TRUSTED source. Sharing is caring.

Good content comes in two forms: other people's content and your original content. Both of these have value to your audience, but what your audience expects will determine the breadth of content you should offer and your optimum ratio of re-posting to original posts.

Other people's content can be found all over the internet on blogs, blog aggregators and expert websites, for instance. Good content gets featured on social media like Facebook, LinkedIn and Twitter.

You can subscribe to blogs and aggregators via RSS to get content delivered in your email or browser. You can create daily Google Alert digests for delivery to your email, or you can choose daily email news tips. Content is everywhere. You just have to search it out, read, follow and confirm it's worthwhile to your audience and share it.

So, what constitutes shareable content? Well, once you've familiarized yourself with copyright fair use principles, what you post depends on your audience. If they are newbies, then look for and share articles or posts that support your methodologies and theories. If your audience consists of your peers and educated clients, you need content that expands horizons, pushes the envelope and questions the norm.

You are not the only person on the internet vying for attention. You are also not everything to everybody. Don't think you have to (or should) post the same content to all your audiences. You may have newbie fans on Facebook and experienced professional connections on LinkedIn. know which audience spends time where and what each craves. Search out intriguing and informative content for each audience and post at the appropriate intervals (neither annoyingly too often nor not often enough to maintain top-of-mind status) to the right audience.

Don't just robo-post

People who use the internet and social media to get their message across have many types of professional and business profiles. Some just want to tell a story, while others want to sell you something. Generally, most fall somewhere in the middle.

The best balance between seeking sales and giving information can be hard to maintain, but needs to be clear in your own mind, because too much selling will drive your hard-won contacts away. You need to know how your audience perceives your information and posts to choose information that makes people to pay attention and act on what you post in the way you want them to.

Educating people can make them ask for more. Give valuable information to someone without expectation of specific return and you can create a fan.

Educating for immediate sale creates skeptics, but may yet lead to some followers and clients. Others will consider your information but resent the selling and look elsewhere for the product or service you offer.

Selling all the time does lead to sales, but the audience that you have a chance to educate about your product or service will dramatically decrease over time.

Over years of posting, watching and learning from others I've grown to recognize these post categories and can predict how people will react to them.

The New Year's Resolution Posts: People make New Year's resolutions to diet, exercise, quit smoking or whatever. They jump right in. But days or weeks later, their enthusiasm has drained away. These kinds of posters hit social media with a rabid fervor, but when they don't see immediate results, they slow down and ultimately fade away. They don't really know who they are or what they want to accomplish and remain completely clueless about what you want!

The Squirrel: Some people gather content like squirrels gather nuts and then spread their gleanings in a burst like shotgun pellets (or squirrel pellets). Although they may find really good stuff, they dilute it worse than a bartender dilutes the liquor on your second drink at a low-budget wedding (apologies to the wedding bartenders and non-drinkers). People may read it, but they don't depend on sources like this.

The In-Law: Others stay away for months and then show up at your doorstep like your mother-in-law (or father-in-law), giving you unsolicited advice on getting the great life he or she has and refusing to leave until you call them the ruler of the world. Then they disappear as fast as they came.

They may try to argue or guilt you into submission. They act like they know something that you don't and give you advice, but then they want you to pay for answers. What they want you to buy is more advice, not real results. Keep your distance.

The Teacher: This type is more concerned about sharing what they know. They expect nothing in return. I know this advice runs counter to nearly every sales book or tape you have ever bought, but it's the most powerful marketing tool you can ever have. You walk a fine line between sharing enough to help people and giving up industry secrets or doing work for free, but you can teach people essential basics without doing their work for them. This type of content-sharer/-producer garners the most followers, fans and (usually) business by far.

Write original content to become a thought leader

Generally, creating original content gets the most people to stand up and take notice. Producing original content with inspirational and engaging thoughts works even better. If you then find ways to get that content noticed and shared and then go viral, you've hit the home run of online marketing.

Email marketing should drive people to your website

Email marketing used to be the preferred method for sharing content. It was simple to use, relatively inexpensive and users responded to it. Today, estimates say 70% of all email traveling across the internet is spam.

People are becoming less and less tolerant of email they really don't want. Computers and networks have become even less tolerant.

In case you're unaware, your general email account from AT&T, Comcast, GMail or another free source limits the number of recipients for mass emails, usually to around 100 recipients at a time. Send to any more than that and your ability to send may be blocked for up to 24 hours. Do this too often and you can be blacklisted.

Once you've been blacklisted, email servers will treat ALL your emails like spam and not deliver even your basic daily emails to single recipients. That's why most people use an email service for their marketing, companies such as Constant Contact, IContact, EmailContact, MailChimp and AWeber. These require KNOW by insisting on Opt-In or Double Opt-In systems, where people can choose to subscribe or unsubscribe to emails. If too many recipients complaint about your mailings, these systems will suspend or delete your account, so prune your lists accordingly.

If you decide to use email as a marketing tool, keep a few things in mind:

1. Even with good email systems, you get limited results. Most research shows a 25% to 35% open rate means you've done well. Click through rates (number of people who click links because of call to action) resemble those for Google Adwords or print advertising, where 2-4% rate is acceptable. If 10% of your total email audience clicks, that's outstanding. For small to medium businesses with 1000-person mailing lists, consider 250-350 opens and 25-35 clicks acceptable.

2. Graphics-heavy emails used to enhance open rates but the overuse of graphics by advertisement emails has made pretty HTML emails look more and more spam-like. Recent trends show movement towards simpler, text-only emails. That's because those look more like personal emails.

3. Think about the way people respond to messaging. The most probable response to an email is to a return email. If you send a text, you are more likely to get a return text. Call someone and leave a voicemail, they will call you back. So if you send a broadcast email, you will get the best response if you ask for an email back, especially if you send a short, simple message that suggests replying to the email as the call to action.

4. If you try to deliver ALL your content through email, chances are you're limiting your effectiveness. Would you have the time or interest to read a 1000-word email? Instead, create enticing teaser-text blurbs that link people to your full content in a blog or on a website.

The most effective use for email marketing? Getting people to click a link for more information. By getting someone to your website, you have the chance to use more detailed text, graphics, audio and video, to enhance their experience. You also increase the chance to generate a sale. The least you could hope for is a phone call or for someone to fill out a 'More Information' form.

Blogs can be a great way to share content
Blogs give you a great way to deliver content because they can be subscribed to, linked to and shared via social

media. Most blog posts run between 300 and 1000 words. They give you an opportunity to share knowledge, insights and tips and tricks that can bring readers back begging for more. I cover blogging in much more detail in Chapter 26.

White papers and ebooks share your ideas and knowledge

Ebooks (or Electronic Books) come in many forms but generally they represent full-length print books that have been converted for e-Readers such as IPads and Kindles. You may even be reading this book (a full-length book available in print) on one of those formats. Business books tend to run between 150 and 300 pages long. Novels tend to start at 250 and go up to 500 pages or more. *War and Peace* runs nearly 1500 pages.

'Special Reports' or 'White Papers' that you deliver through websites as PDF downloads also serve as marketing tools, but can be shorter. Many places use pdf download permissions to ask you for your email information or to sign up for email newsletters. And although the shorter documents should also be protected by copyright laws, full ebooks more often claim "rights protected," meaning they limit sharing to protect revenue streams. Marketers intend their reports or white papers for sharing freely, promoting your content to the widest possible audience.

There are several advantages to using electronic marketing documents:

- You can write less than a full book, maybe only a few chapters' wortha few pages to maybe 100 pages.

- You can afford to include more graphics than most printed books, giving you the opportunity to build your brand.

- They can be freely shared, spreads your expert content and name

- They can easily be updated by rewriting and re-uploading.

The negatives are that you do NOT control sharing with these eMarketing documents. If your main goal is gathering names for a list, you can ask for it in the document, but you can't count on people honoring your request. You also cannot prevent others from copying and pasting your content into their own marketing materials and self-branding. You can easily export text from PDFs in a copy-able, paste-able format. After a little re-formatting, the source disappears. Copyrights are only enforceable if you can find the misuse, prove it and have enough money to protect it.

With that said, ebooks can still give you a great way to promote your knowledge, business and brand. Some companies produce dozens of ebooks to promote various services and concepts that help potential consumers get to know their brand and business better. These companies may use the ebooks to gather new names, but they also actively promote new ebooks to current subscribers with the hope that this next ebook will convert a contact into a customer, advocate, or reseller. How might your business use simple ebooks to promote your business or your brand?

However you choose to deliver your great content, be sure to keep it them–focused, remembering the wants and needs of your target audience. You should have two main goals: to create a buzz about you and your business and to create a perception that they should trust you as an expert or resource.

Social networking may be the only tool in your arsenal, but it could be a good proving ground before you start to explore more expensive and time-consuming options. Seeing how people respond and interact in social media can serve as a good barometer for what types of content people really crave.

CHAPTER 26: BLOGGING

BACON-IZMS

- Blogs can be hosted on free accounts

- Your blog should be an extension of your business

- Never sell through your blog

- Know the rules

- Keep blog posts to 300-500 words

- Good headlines grab attention

- Personality can increase connection

- Pictures can increase interaction

- Include a call to action

- Use bulleted lists

- Write about what your audience wants to read

- Build your audience

Blogging has been around for years. Originally known as Web Logs, the practice has become mainstream and easier than ever to set up and maintain. It's even changing the way that websites are being set up.

Blogs can be hosted on free accounts

You can find many free blog platform choices, including Blogger (from Google), Blog.com, Tumbler and WordPress. Blogger and Wordpress are the most popular because they offer users the most flexibility and power.

I am a big fan of WordPress and so are a lot of internet marketers and webmasters. You have two choices when setting up a WordPress blog. The free version, which includes hosting, is at wordpress.com. You simply sign up and WordPress starts the blog for you. The plus is that it's easy to set up and you need do little or no site maintenance (as opposed to content development). The down side is that your web traffic gets associated with the Wordpress.com and does little or nothing to promote your brand with search engines. Your free web address will be yourbiz.wordpress.com.

One of the most powerful things about WordPress blogs is the opportunity they offer you to add themes (for look and feel) and plug-ins or widgets (programs that add functionality). Most are free, although some are paid-for extras. The free version of WordPress does not offer all possible options. So, short version: WordPress has limitations, but if you need a simple, free way to create a blog, it's a great option.

WordPress is also available as a free download from wordpress.org. This is software that you can install on your own web server. This option is included with hosting accounts from HostGator, BlueHost, GoDaddy and many other web hosting platforms. Although those companies have simple auto-install options, the process is not always as simple as it seems. It helps if you have some skills and knowledge of php, cascading style sheets (css), mysql, html and other web technologies. If you don't, hook up with one of the techies in your area or networking groups and employ one to help you with installation, upgrades and maintenance. And don't let a more complex start-up process deter you. I have set up and trained hundreds (some very non-techie) on how to update and maintain WordPress blog sites themselves.

Even if you choose to use the free version from wordpress.com first, one of the major advantages is that you can export the blog and data and import into a self-hosted option later. Having the ability to upgrade and extend the capabilities of your blog or website is a huge advantage, an investment in your business' future.

Another advantage of using a WordPress self-hosted option is the ability to create a fully functional website known as a blog site. Not every blog site has to have a blog, by the way, but you'll have the option to add that at any time.

With theme options from Theme Forrest, Elegant Themes, Woo Themes and many others, you have the ability to make your website look and feel as good as any other website programming options available. These themes also give you the functionality to change the look and feel of your website at any time, without having to start from scratch.

If you already have a static-HTML website log, you can upload WordPress into a subfolder and add a blog that way as well.

Other alternatives include Drupal and Joomla CMS (content management system) platforms. They are often much more powerful than other blogging platforms. They give you the ability to build completely unique websites and blog sites, but also take a higher level of technical skill and knowledge to update and maintain.

You have many choices and options when it comes to blogging. You'll need to make some choices, but none more important than the one committing you to blogging.

Your blog should be an extension of your business

So now that we have the technical appetizer course done, let's get to the entrée. Blogging is about creating content meant to be read, shared and commented upon. It's all about creating interaction and KNOW/LIKE/TRUST connections.

Blog content ranges from what you are going through in your life, to political opinions, to tips and tricks, to rants and raves, to reviews and pans, to anything you could possibly imagine. Some of the most powerful blogs cover dealing with medical conditions, parenting, and family life. Some of the most controversial deal with politics. But remember, what matters for your blog is, who is your audience and what do they want to hear about and discuss? It's Not About You... it's about them.

What you choose to blog about depends on your goals as well. Are you trying to position yourself as a trainer or expert? Do you want to build an audience of like-minded professionals or hobbyists? Are you trying change or formulate opinions? Your audience will tell you whether you've succeeded or not!

Write about what your audience wants to read

What makes a blog successful? It starts with excellent content. Now you may be like me, someone who says, "I am not a writer, so how will anyone care what I have to say?"

Well, I started out blogging about my iPhone and apps. My writing, grammar and the organization of my blog were all awful. Yet many readers looked past that, read them and commented. Since then, I've built a nice audience. Over the years, my blog has morphed into a tool that enhances my classes, presentations—and my business!

What could you blog about? The easiest topics come from your experience of your business or industry that could teach others. You could give lessons learned or best practices, debunk myths, list important truths, or anything else new, informative or thought-provoking. The best blogs happen when you raise questions that evoke comments and interactions.

Know the rules

Just as with Art, a good blog is in the eye of the beholder, but if you know the rules, you can turn an OK blog into a good blog or a good blog into a great one. These techniques may not all work equally well with every industry, nor should you take them as the ultimate authority, but they do hold across most of the blogosphere.

I suggest you find some rock stars in your industry and look at what formulas they use. Start using their formulas and then tweak them to invent your own—so others can follow you. No one owns the right to, or will forever have the best formula for, the perfect blog. That's always up to your audience.

Keep blog posts to 300-500 words

To determine the best length for a blog, first consider your audience's attention span. Too much content means people stop reading after a while because they never have time to finish your posts. Give too little and you leave them feeling unsatisfied: questions unanswered, points not explained.

Don't make the mistake of thinking that your blog can work as teaser text to drive people to your website for more detail. That can easily backfire if people resent not getting the whole story on the first page where they land. Also, Google currently likes content that is least 300 words and therefore, so do blog aggregators. They want Google's attention and so do you. So in most cases, you should make 300 words the minimum length for posts.

On the other hand, less is more above that 300 words. Don't try to explain in too much detail. Look at what you have to say and decide how much will be too much, generally anything over 500-1000 words. If you have to cut out key content and points to reach that upper limit, your post should probably be at least two posts. Possibly even one post for every point you want to make.

Each blog post should follow its own flow. Let you message and the intended audience be your length police. Remember, you lose the reader who doesn't ever have the time or attention span to finish.

Good headlines grab attention

As a student of advertising and marketing, I have found that one of the most powerful things you can do is craft excellent headlines. Great headlines draw people into reading more. Why do you think newspapers, magazines and advertising have employed writers and editors who specialize in headline creation?

Blogs are no different. You need your headlines to alert people to a problem, offer a solution... or both!

- "Why Treats from China Are Bad for Your Pet!"

- "Is Your 401K... Really O.K.?"

- "Five Common Mistakes When Opening Your Family Pool for the Season!"

Headlines need to be short. If they don't fit in a tweet, they're too long. They should also grab people's emotions and be action-driven and problem/solution-based to garner the most attention. Think of your headline as your blog post's slogan. If you strike a chord with a solution or cleverly define a problem and it emotionally connects with audiences, you will be rewarded with posts, comments, shares and re-tweets!

Whatever the topic, you have to grab your audience to get them to read your content. Once you draw them in, you owe them payback with awesome content.

Personality can increase connections

Remember textbooks? Generally boring and impersonal, right? If you want to create a connection, you have to insert your personality, experiences and flaws or successes into your posts. People can tell the difference between a set script and pouring your heart out. Share anecdotes, tell stories, or use real life experiences to make your blog stand out from the hundreds, if not thousands, of other people offering similar information.

Use a perspective that people can relate to. Don't put your family or anyone's secrets in jeopardy, but put your personality on the line. Napoleon Hill, who wrote Think and Grow Rich, was not the first person to write a success manual. Sun Tzu was not the first to write about The Art of War and Tony Robbins was not the first person to write a self-help book. You recognize their names because they each wrote with a unique perspective on some very basic and time-proven principles.

Pictures can increase interaction

If you have watched the evolution of the blog and the internet, and especially social media, you've seen that pictures have moved from absent to center stage. Facebook, LinkedIn and even Twitter (with only its 140 characters) have all gotten more visual, primarily due to the growth of websites like Flickr and Pinterest, developed to feature visuals.

Pictures draw people in and enhance your messages. The simplest way is take your own pictures and import them. Otherwise you have to rely on stock or clip art. Don't try to just search Google for pics and repost because you may run into costly copyright issues. Refer to Chapter 17, on creative rights, for more on this subject,but don't let that deter you from using pictures for a visual connection with your well-written content!

Include a call to action

You've told your story or made your argument. Now what? Ask people to do something. True, the harder you sell, the more you risk pushing people away. However, if you don't include some type of call to action, people will just move on to the next infosource, which may hard-sell them into submission.

So, challenge them act on your advice. Have them try your techniques and email you about how they worked. Ask for comments on your post All these create interaction.

The bottom line is, if you don't ask, people will do nothing. Of course, even if you do ask, people may still do nothing. You have to have a plan in mind and have realistic expectations. The one thing that may not work for you is sending them to another location with a call-to-action link. The one thing that gets the most interaction? Asking people for comments, feedback or opinions.

Calls to action need to be subtle and sincere. Messages on websites and in blogs and emails overwhelm people with instructions, leaving many numb to calls to action. You have to deliver outstanding content and a compelling reason to act for them to pay attention to your call to action.

Use bulleted lists

Did you notice how many bulleted lists and numbered lists I've included in this book? People love lists for some reason. Remember the Book of Lists or the Guinness Book of World Records? People like order.

Lists also create limits on what you need to do:

- Three Steps to Success

- Five of the Latest Fashion Trends

- Four New Lawn Care Concerns

Because of that, numbers that suggest lists also show up in titles of popular songs, movies and books, such as "You're Once, Twice, Three Times a Lady," 3 Easy Pieces, and any 12-Step Plan.

No one can guarantee that the list trend will continue forever, but you can be reassured that this marketing and communication methodology has seen use over hundreds of years now!

Never sell through your blog

The only thing you cannot do with blogging is sell. People are not going to comment, share or interact, when all you try to do is sell them something. It's a huge mistake to treat blogging like a big broadcast email. People may read it once or twice, but fill it with spam-like copy and any subscribers will unsubscribe Others will just plain ignore it. It's Not About You...

Beyond not selling, what you should not post about depends on your audience and the size of the audience you want to reach. Some people are content to talk only with their friends and family, to whom what they ate for lunch, where they shop and what their cat does may be interesting. But this won't interest a broad audience.

OK, one just like that called "Shit My Dad Says" by Justin Halpern became a huge internet success. It saw such a success that it got made into a (failed) TV show. But that's a rare exception.

Some people talk politics and find huge audiences. You see thousands of successful political blogs out there. But political blogs alienate 50% of their possible audience, which may not work well for your business.

Understand, I can give you no absolute right and wrong answers here. As long as you are knowledgeable and passionate about your topic, your blog can find an audience. How large an audience is the next question.

Build Your Audience

Just putting a blog out there is a start. If it gets enough traffic, it will start to show up in search engines... but on what page? A few tools can help spread the word about your blog and help you build an audience.

Most blogs have RSS (rich site summary or, as it's often called, real simple syndication) included in the blogging tool. This generally converts your blog posts to a feed that can be read in browsers or emails programs. Users can subscribe to the feed by clicking the RSS icon on the site, or by subscribing via a URL (usually feed.yourwebsite.com).

RSS allows multiple sources (Facebook, Twitter and others) to read your feed and post on your behalf. Often this requires a third party plug-in or app. Others, like LinkedIn, have removed the subscription app to discourage robo-posting and encourage you to actually sign in to copy and paste posts, thus improving their site's interactivity.

Another option is a Google tool called FeedBurner that allows people to subscribe via email and delivers your blog to their inbox. FeedBurner helpfully reports some stats to you, such as how many people subscribe and how engaged they are with your content. Simply go to feedburner.google.com and set up an account. If you already have a Google or GMail account the process is simple and seamless. After you set up your account, you will be provided with some code that you can cut-and-paste into a blog page or a text widget.

Next, you should explore the world of blog aggregators. These sites have the ability to read your RSS feed and then post items to their websites. With most of these, you have to register, set up an account, and then be approved to be included in their website feed. Literally thousands of options exist, so check what's relevant for your purposes. Some of the most popular are Reddit, Technorati and StumbleUpon. These tend to be fairly broad in scope, which means users have to choose which topics they want to receive. Depending on your topic or industry, you could see anything from dozens to millions of competing posts per day.

If you can find some industry-specific blog aggregators, you may have an easier time finding and building an audience. Some of these will simply grab your feeds and repost them. Others will review them, posting some when appropriate. A few of them will ask you to actually create original content, which they will publish on your behalf.

I have had posts published by Business2Community. com. On their website, they offer users the ability to share via social media or comment. This means I get the chance to respond to the comments directly. Aggregators like this can take a blog which reaches hundreds through my website and present it to a larger audience, giving all of them a chance to comment and share with still others. If any of them redistribute the post to their Facebook and Twitter accounts, it can go even further. Some of my posts have shown up on the Yahoo Small Business Advisor website.

That is just one example of how simple yet compelling blog posts can go from reaching hundreds to tens of thousands of views, all with your business associated to it and most linking back to your website.

If you want to see this at work, follow people in your industry on Twitter or look up blogs on Technorati, Reddit or Stumble Upon. See how others do it and learn!

Bringing It Home

Back to the original points about which blogging platform to use. If you do something that points a lot of people back to your blog, how beneficial do you think it would be to have your website and other marketing materials wrapped around that?

Having a blog that is read and shared is awesome. Having a blog with tons of traffic that is tied to and drives tons of traffic to your website is more awesome. If someone comes to your blog to read a post and sees links to your services and testimonials and then clicks on them, it's internet gold.

If you can generate a web inquiry, phone call or email from your blog and ultimately a sale, that is why blogging is so important! Blogs are simply just an awesome way so share your knowledge, get others to engage and promote your business on the internet!

CHAPTER 27: TOGETHERNESS

BACON-IZMS

- Great content gets shared

- Going viral can happen to you

- Create a tribe or community around content

- Use other communities to spread your messages

- Search out opportunities to share your messages

Great content gets shared

Creating great content is only one way to promote your business. Getting others to share your great content is the challenge. Part of relationship marketing is getting people with whom you have formed relationships to like, comment on and share your messages.

I was interviewed for an Entrepreneur magazine article about when is the best time to tweet. My answer? For me and my clients, 7, 8, 9 and 10 a.m. and 4, 5, 6 and 7 p.m. Central Daylight Time. Why? In Chicago, where I live, that covers prime commuter time across all four time zones in the continental US. That's when traffic is hottest on Twitter because people are going to and coming from work, or checking in at the beginning or the end of the work day.

When you share information can be as important as what you are sharing. If your audience is businesspeople, you are better off sharing when they are at their desks at work. If you do business with consumers, you may have better luck sharing content Friday night and Saturday morning, before they've made or when they're making the decision on where to shop this weekend.

Traditionally, advertising flyers came in the Sunday newspaper because that was when the most people had the time to read the whole newspaper, but the internet has changed things. Just as your Sunday paper is no longer thicker than your average phone book, Sunday may not be when you need to reach your audience!

Think about when the content that you're posting has the best opportunity to be read... because that is the best time for you to share it!

Going viral can happen to you

I worked with Juliana Vinson of Cell-Parts.net to revitalize the company (then called simply Cell Parts) that her grandfather started in 1944. The company makes one simple product: a ferrule, the small piece of plastic that sits on a golf club between the shaft and the hosel (the socket of a golf club head into which the shaft fits).

Thomas V. Dorr, a passionate golfer, not only wanted to improve his game, but to enhance the golfing experience for others as well. He enjoyed playing golf with pros and entertainers alike. He created a special plastic so crack-resistant that almost every golf-club manufacturer in

America purchased their ferrules from Cell Parts. The business enjoyed decades of success and growth.

Juliana approached me after a class I'd taught and said, "I need help!" Grandpa had died and the business had slowly scaled down to only a handful of employees. The problem? From the late 1990s into the early 2000s, all the golf-club manufacturers had moved their business to China, where clubs could be manufactured for pennies on the dollar, creating huge profits for the industry. Although her parts only cost 7¢/piece, orders dried up. She now faced some hard choices.

She'd managed to get a government grant to help small business that had lost business to competitors overseas. It was about enough to cover a few months' mortgage payments but had to be spent on promoting to new markets. Thus Juliana asked for my help. I honestly was not sure if or how I could help but we managed to keep her company buoyant long enough for business to start coming back.

This project had three phases, which involved answering three key questions:

- What was the ferrule and what did it mean to golf?

- Who was the potential audience to buy it?

- How could we promote it to re-build the business?

Part one involved research. I contacted club pros, wholesalers and golfers, anyone connected to golf. I asked them, "What does a ferrule do and why is it important to you?" The basic answer was, it's just a decorative piece of plastic that hides the juncture where the shaft goes into the hosel (the golf club head).

That all sounded kind of disappointing until Juliana put me in touch with a client who works with the top golf professionals. He told me that he was the shaft master to the pros and he worked with almost everyone. For the same reason that you want a pool cue to be straight, he ran a business that re-shafted clubs at almost every major golf tournament.

Since I am a golfer, I could understand that having the right shaft, or right grips, on club heads that you are promoting can make be a million-dollar decision in a golf tournament, even though most observers would not know the difference!

And then I learned the priceless part. He said, "I don't care if that little piece of plastic cost 7¢ or $7. It's a decorative piece—until it breaks. Juliana's ferules are so far superior to the others that I would pay anything. If that little piece of plastic breaks, it costs me $50 to $100 to fix the club. I am not willing to take that chance!"

Part two involved re-defining the audience. Juliana realized that she could make ferules in colors in ways that others could not match, especially with her quality being so far superior. We decided to produce ferrules in colors of popular schools and sports teams for marketing to hobbyists. Rather than sell them for 7¢/piece in bulk, we could potentially sell them for $1 or more each to fanatics. Trust me, changing to that approach took a hard sell to Juliana and her family and staff.

Part three took re-inventing their business on the web. We created a new website. The old one focused on the golf club companies, who had wanted to know about the technology of manufacturing. The new one focuses on consumers. It tells the history of the company and explains their ability to customize your golf clubs with cool new ferules. We hired a photographer to take the pictures to help us promote the new ferrules to our targeted audience.

We show the colors and options and explain how special-ists and hobbyists can do something new and exciting. The one challenge left to deal with? Hardly anyone knew about this company and the options it offered.

So, we venture onto the golf-club building and hobbyist forums to promote the brand and the website. The posts read something like this, "Check out this new website that lets you customize ferules for you own golf clubs!" Initially, everyone said, "Spammer, Go away!" But when people started commenting on my comment, I started seeing responses like, "Wait, I have used Cell-Parts ferules. They are the best and the real deal!" The opinion turnaround started to snowball and traffic to the website started to escalate!

A day or so later, I got a phone call from Juliana. She said, "I don't know what the hell you did, but you are killing me! I am so busy answering the phone and emails that I don't have any time to get work done!"

What we did was re-invent the business in a way that became viral. It was the enthusiasts that continued to promote the business into success again.

Juliana called again a few years later. She said that the new approach could not replace the millions of ferules they'd sold to the golf club companies, but had helped sustain the company for a while. Long enough that they and club manufacturers discovered what the shaft whisperer had learned. The cost of replacing that 7¢ part was costing $100 a club when it was shipped to the company to fix when it broke! Because of that, golf-club companies were coming back to them, to get the high-quality, proprietary polymers that made Cell-Parts' ferules great.

The point here is that, even if you produce the best product in the world (literally), you may need social media marketing to sustain you through startup or propel you beyond what traditional marketing can only hope to accomplish!

Create a tribe or community around content

You've just read about the power of community. The golf-club-building enthusiasts who commented did so out of shared love for the company's quality, excellent customer service and creative options. The conversation went viral and continues to bring in customers today.

You need community to help you spread your messages and content. Part of building a relationship-based network involves creating and nurturing an emotional connection between them and you and from there, with your business. If you provide your audience with excellent content, they will share what touches them with their followers, thus amplifying your ability to reach a broad audience.

You can't just expect that community to broadcast your messages with reach out to them through comments on, likes for and shares of their messages. You need to seem like part of THEIR community before they'll return the favor with YOUR messages! Being an active part of community will lead to results.

People talk, a lot. Either you take part in the conversation, or YOU ARE the topic of conversation. You can't get away with simply posting your own stuff without ever liking or commenting on other people's posts. You need to be part of the conversation, which also means liking and commenting on everyone's responses to your posts. If you get negative responses, try to set up a direct message sidebar conver-sation to smooth out the problems people may have with you and your business.

If you are a small or regional business, people expect YOU to communicate on the web, as a person not a corporate entity. People want to know that you are real and have a life, just like them. Only posting on a business page can seem like white noise. Worse yet, using your personal profile as a business profile is not only against Facebook user agreements, but the fastest way to get hidden or de-friended!

Having and using a personal profile in a personal way holds your key to success on Facebook. Talk about your pets, hobbies and other things that create human connections. When you're only all about business, your message just gets boring!

If you want to alienate at least 50% of your audience, then go ahead, post your views on religion and politics. Nobody is telling you not to HAVE beliefs, values or opinions, but you run a risk when sharing them on social media. In business, you need to stay neutral. Whether you are conservative or liberal, pro- or anti-anything, limit sharing opinions on those subjects to your personal and offline conversations. Broadcasting your beliefs, opinions, or rants to the world could lead to lost business.

You also cannot expect to have impact as a mere consumer of information. You need to find or create content that creates responses, likes and comments. You need to work hard at it and monitor the feedback. Don't be offended if what you post gets little or no response, just try harder. Expect nothing in return and you will never be disappointed.

I have hit many duds, while some other posts bring the desired result by going viral with more than 1000 shares and 100,000 views. Talk about spreading the word about your business!

Most people don't ask their first date to marry them, but that's how some people treat social media. They think that just posting a few messages should yield results.

Relationships take time to mature. You may wait years to see predictable, measurable results.

Be patient; continue learning what enhances your relationship with fans and followers. Don't be afraid to ask friends and colleagues what they do and don't like. Do more of what works, less of what does not, and LEARN to know the difference.

Use other communities to spread your messages

In the section on blogging, I talked briefly about blog aggregators. I revisit them here, along with a range of other approaches for connecting with communities beyond your won to spread your message.

Blogs and Aggregators: Besides writing your own blog and registering with the aggregators, you can find tons of blogs that are hungry for content. You can either be a guest blogger, or an industry expert for an interview. Some blogs look for quick 50-word-or-less tip lists, while others will accept (or prefer) full-length articles. My client John Nachtrieb from BarCode-Test LLC gets featured as a contributor on BarCode.com often. Even print magazines may need online-only content.

Being part of other people's media posts is another great way to promote your brand and business. In Chapter 13, I mentioned two great resources to help you find places where people will ask you to share your knowledge, experience and expertise:

Help A Reporter Out (helpareporter.com): a website where you can sign up and get daily emails about writers and sources that are looking for people to help them with their content.

Reporter Connection (reporterconnection.com): a similar source with reporters looking for experts.

Both of these offer multiple venues for you to share your knowledge or content.

Print and Magazines: Newspapers and magazines are hungry for content as well. You may need to hire a public relations professional to generate press releases telling your story, but it can be money well spent. Search out writers for local papers and try to connect with them. I have had the opportunity to be included in articles for Inc. and Entrepreneur magazines, national trade publications and tons of local news stories. Building your brand in print can be a huge boost for your business.

Radio Interviews and Podcasts: Locate some of the dozens of radio stations and thousands of programs that cover your field of business by searching podcasts in ITunes. You will be amazed at the amount of content being generated there.

Sites like BlogTalkRadio.com let anyone create their own radio show and podcast. People using them want to interview people who have knowledge and expertise in specific fields and industries.

Can't find what you are looking for? Maybe it's time for you to try to be the broadcaster or reporter. Blog-TalkRadio.com will let you schedule your own internet broadcast for free. You can produce a daily, weekly or monthly podcast and upload it to your website and sites like ITunes. Producing podcasts runs beyond the scope of this book, but it's something for you to consider.

TV and Cable: I personally have a face for radio, but you may be the next celebrity expert that local or nationally syndicated shows are looking for. And don't discount exposure on local cable TV stations. If you get a good interview, you can obtain the rights to post links, or the entire video, on your own website to enhance your brand or reputation as an expert.

Any help spreading your brand is good, but try to ensure that, when you do get press, coverage links back to your website or blog. Also, be aware that some people will actually charge you to be interviewed or recorded. I try to avoid these, but you may think the cost is worthwhile to get well-produced content that you can share on your website or across social media.

Use as many options as possible to help spread the word about your business. Yes, it's work, but the payback can far outweigh your time on task.

CHAPTER 28:
WHAT'S YOUR BACON?

BACON-IZMS

- What's your bacon?

- What makes you YOU?

- Don't fake it

- Nurture a community that helps share your bacon

- Make your Bacon sizzle

- Go gourmet with your Bacon

- Your audience will tell you when you do it right

By now, you should know the mantra of the Bacon brand: It's Not About You, It's About (fill in the blank). Relationship marketing in a social media world is about dealing with business and networking on a human level.

Thousands of books cover prospecting, cold calling, and generating and closing sales. Those all have a place in running a successful business. Programs and software tools can help you benchmark and measure effectiveness, create methodologies that build psychological profiles of buyers and otherwise motivate you to approach the challenge of promoting your business like a sports pro playing the biggest game of your life. And yet, while these all have their value and place, if you spend all your time prepping, measuring and pumping yourself up for sales, you may miss why people actually buy from you—why they KNOW, LIKE and TRUST you. They do this because you connect with them and treat them like a human being, not like a mere prospect or sale!

What does it mean to be human? It means that you have a family, a life and a personality that is not built around 60-second commercials, tag lines and sales pitches. You can take your kids to soccer, baseball, basketball, tae kwon do, or tennis. You play piano, act, paint, make pottery or quilts. You volunteer or run a committee for a local nonprofit. You like music, movies, fishing, golf, wine, or Thai food. What makes you you? What could be a connector to others? What's your Bacon?

What's your bacon?

Your Bacon is anything about you that makes you memorable or keeps you top of mind. It's the thing that creates an opportunity to reach others through conversations, connections and commonalities. You probably have multiple Bacons, multiple places to connect with people. You may connect with one group on one level (beginner) and another group on a different level (expert). The more Bacons you can identify, the better chance you have to build a relationship.

Some people have restrictions on how they can communicate. For instance, I have taught, consulted for and presented to more than one financial professional. SEC restrictions limit financial professionals regarding what they can post and what platforms they can use.

Most cannot use Facebook for business. They can use LinkedIn, but cannot receive recommendations. Those limits on their professional life exist so they cannot be perceived as giving advice on investment online, which might constitute insider trading.

Because of those restrictions, a financial advisor asked me, "What can social networking do for me?"

I asked him what his hobbies were and he said he loved sailing. I suggested he let that be his Bacon. He could use a personal profile on Facebook or LinkedIn to join or start groups about sailing. Then he could connect with other sailing enthusiasts and talk about his passion. He could be perceived as a resource and a trusted advisor regarding his hobby, sailing. As long as he does not use online tools to sell financial advice, he has no other restrictions. If he gets the opportunity to meet with some of his connections face to face, then he already has KNOW and LIKE covered and can work in person on getting to the TRUST level.

What makes you YOU?

I have many passions. My Bacons include music, golf, community, sports teams, computers and much more. This huge array of Bacon options lets me create different connections with different groups. I call my golfing 'Fore Hour Nature Meetings.' I take pictures of my band playing. I post commentary about and pictures of my favorite sports teams.

Online connections are just an extension of real-life relationships. As you should now see, you too can interact with people on an emotional level in many ways that create conversations, connections and commonalities. Just being who you are you often interests others much more that what you do for a living or what you sell. It amazes me how often people ignore that and use social media as a sales tool.

This does not mean that you can just follow people and try to piggyback on their passions. More than one person has been called out for being a fair-weather fan to lure others into creating connections. Just saying "Go Hawks" when someone is talking about their favorite sports team does not create a connection. In fact, it may turn someone off by branding you as a bandwagon jumper.

Another thing to use sparingly if at all is polarizing content. If you post political or religious views or opinions (especially controversial ones), you could anger 50% of your audience. No one is telling you not to be yourself, or telling you to change your convictions or belief system, but be careful about how you present them in a public forum such as Facebook, LinkedIn, Twitter, or Pinterest. You may never hear why directly, but more than one person has lost business because of what they posted online. Be supportive and positive; avoid being divisive and negative.

Don't fake it

By the way, don't be fooled by Turkey Bacon. We all know that turkey bacon is not real bacon. It's marketed as a healthier alternative to pork bacon, but it's still a substitute, not the real thing. The same goes for social networking. People can tell whether you're selling a Bacon substitute or offering to share samples of the real thing!

I am sure you've had people try to buddy up to you just for your knowledge or to win your business. I am sure you have had people who tried to use you for free services or advice. I am certain that you have been taken advantage of in business. It does not feel good and could make you downright angry.

So the best thing you can do is remember what that feels like and don't try to do it to others. Be yourself. Share your passions without expectations. Give of your knowledge and experience anyway, unafraid that people might try to take advantage. Know what your Bacon is and just be you. Be the BACON!

Nurture a community that helps share your bacon

Once you've identified your Bacon, provide original and re-purposed content that creates conversations. Original can include your blogs, pictures and simple posts. Re-purposed can include shares from other posts and groups, copied links and videos.

The key choice factor for you should be, what does your audience interact with? Some groups love pictures while others like videos. Some may like quotes, while other appreciate articles gleaned from the web. There is no one right answer and answers can change over time.

It's up to you to keep an eye on what generates the most likes and shares. Do more of what works and less of what doesn't. It's Not About You... It's about your audience!

Quality content is the cornerstone of creating engagement in social media. I have seen companies like Smart Dogs Training post pictures of dogs who've graduated from their programs. They gather dozens of likes and comments with pictures of them in a graduation cap! But I have also seen experts post links to great content that gets no likes or comments. Beauty (or quality) is in the eye of the beholder and viewers will vote with their interactions.

People will tell you when just sharing your passion is not enough. They want to feel a connection that creates interaction. Otherwise you just become more white noise. And trust me, there is a LOT of white noise out there.

Make your Bacon sizzle

Do you remember seeing (or doing) The Wave at sporting events? People would synchronize standing up, waving their arms and sitting back down. The motion would move across the sections of the stadium like a wave and made quite a spectacle to see from the Goodyear blimp. Creating a viral response in social media comes from synchronous reactions something like this.

You'll know when you have struck a chord that resonates, when people go beyond just liking or commenting. People post pictures and links on your social media and start to mention you. You will know when you have started a digital wave. Not only are your posts top of mind, but when others see content that enhances the conversation, they post it and mention you in it.

Let's say you knit. If people see some cool knitting project, they may share that on your timeline and start conversations for you. This can pull all of their friends and connections into the conversation. Now your social media presence is starting to grow, to engage people outside your immediate network. When this happens, you know you have gone from simply building relationships to building a broader sphere of influence!

Go gourmet with your Bacon

You can't just re-purpose other people's ideas and hope that you are going to make an impact. You also can't just be a news reporter. You have to be making news, too. You have to create original content with thought-provoking ideas to create conversations, especially if you want people to share your content, hoping some of it will go viral.

I mentioned before that going viral truly is like catching lightning in a bottle. But you can't catch lightning unless you stand out in a few storms. That means you have to be willing to challenge the status quo and challenge conventional thinking.

Not everybody has to agree with you, but you certainly don't want to be so far left (or right) of center that all you get is criticism and dissension! You also don't want to be so plain vanilla that you sound like you're always copying other people.

You have to offer new and creative insight that makes people want to comment or share. Think Different is more than just an Apple slogan, it's what people look for in the sea of white noise that floods the internet, blogs and social media every day!

The underlying goal is to be the person people think of when they need what you do or sell. Get them to KNOW, LIKE and TRUST you through something other than your business. Then, when you also post kudos for a client, or even news about a business accomplishment, they will be more likely to pay attention and even respond.

So you don't need to talk only about your Bacon. You can mention your business, just not all the time. Get people to connect with you on a personal level and they will be much more comfortable and inclined to connect with you on a business level.

Your audience will tell you when you do it right

Relationships are valuable and fragile assets. You have to water them, feed them and nurture them. Finding your Bacon, sharing your Bacon and getting others interested in your Bacon clearly takes time and commitment.

People are people. The more you remember that in business, the better chance you have to be successful. This is true for everyone: employees, vendors, power partners, friends, family, neighbors, clients and prospective clients. Being yourself and sharing your personal passions, pastimes and preferences can go a long way to getting people to KNOW, LIKE and TRUST you on a professional level.

CHAPTER 29: IT'S A WRAP!

BACON-IZMS

- Marketing is a journey

- Technology and the internet change daily

- Where can I learn about this stuff?

- Start with Google

- Find good resources to learn from

- Keep on learning

- Be the Bacon

Marketing is a Journey

By now I hope you have learned a few new things. Just writing this book was a learning experience for me. I tried to present a lot of practical and useful information. Chances are, you found a few new concepts you think will help you, confirmed a few of your hunches and had a few treasured myths debunked.

Most importantly, I hope you have learned, re-learned or confirmed that relationships are one of your most valuable assets in business. They need to be started, watered and carefully cultivated. They form the cornerstone of success for most entrepreneurs.

Technology and the internet change daily

In Chapter 2, right at the beginning of the book, I talked about how change has affected every aspect of our businesses and particularly how we plan, execute, manage and grow them.

Just a few short decades ago, we felt liberated when we could transfer our vinyl albums to cassettes and jog around listening to an audiocassette Walkman. In 2001, the first hard-drive-based IPod, that all changed. The IPod drive could hold 1000 songs and cost $399. As this book goes to press, you can buy a flash memory version that holds 500 songs for only $49. Who knows what's next?

Social networking is relatively young as well. Facebook, founded in 2004, was not yet around when the first IPod hit the market. Eight years later, Facebook had ballooned to more than 1 billion users. The IPod has evolved into the IPhone, into which Facebook is fully integrated. Social media really only became mainstream on a few years ago. Who knows what these platforms will do and look like, or if they will even exist in the same forms in few more years.

Where can I learn about this stuff?

I'm ending this book the same way I end every one of the classes I teach. Some of these classes are three-hour concept-spewing marathons that overwhelm attendees with information. You see the same glazed look in each student's eyes. One of the best questions people ask is, "Where can I learn more about this stuff?" The most direct and ironic answer? "Google It!"

Start with Google

Things change daily, but we're given a huge community of very educated and energetic people out on the Web who are learning, trying, blogging and teaching from trial and error and experience. If you go looking, you'll find a lot of their knowledge being chronicled across the internet every day.

Find good resources to learn from

Find good resources like Mashable, Technorati, Business-2Community, or whatever web and blog aggregator offers you the most useful and current information that is relevant to your industry.

Keep on learning

Whatever you learn today is the foundation on which you can learn tomorrow, but you should never stop learning. The principles about relationships in this book may be timeless, but the parts about social networking and social media are completely fluid.

Who knows what tomorrow will bring? At any moment. change can happen, giving a completely new form and function to any social networking property. Or the next new thing can replace it entirely. Even what we KNOW, LIKE and TRUST today can simply disappear.

It's up to you to jumping into the fray and then do your best to spend as much time as possible learning. Some of the learning can be free, other options you may need to pay for. But it's up to you to search out the best social media and network marketing options for you and your business.

Use your newly found friends and communities to ask questions and ask for help. They are there just waiting for you to do that; they want to help you. Reciprocate by being there for them, too. Be a resource for people who follow you into the fray.

Be the Bacon

Try your best to become a good and active member of all of your communities, both online and offline. Be a resource at the same time as you're soaking up more knowledge. Take your chance to learn, grow and pay it forward!

If you found what I've written of value and a good use of your time, pass this book on. Teach someone else what you have learned and, most of all, pay it forward. You will be rewarded by the people who get to KNOW, LIKE and TRUST you.

It's Not About You, It's About Being the BACON!

ABOUT THE BACONOLOGIST

Brian Basilico is a nationally recognized social media expert and speaker. He is the Director of Direction at B2b Interactive Marketing, his company that combines audio, video, interactive, web communications, and advertising to improve clients' marketing and exposure.

Brian leverages more than three decades worth of experience in the communications industry to help his clients with their advertising and marketing needs. He's done sound and video work for Fortune 500 companies such as AT&T and Arthur Andersen. He's a seasoned producer, developer, and marketer with experience in everything from CD-Rom production to the most modern social media and SEO trends.

From an early age, Brian put his love for music and entrepreneurial spirit into overdrive. At the age of 2 he strummed a broomstick and shook his hips like Elvis. By 10 he was playing the guitar, and in his teenage years, he purchased a $1,000 4-track recorder—the eventual catalyst to a half-a-million-dollar recording studio business.

He lives in the Chicago suburbs with his wife Kim and their Black Lab, Buddy Guy. In addition to his love for marketing and music, he continues to explore his abnormal obsession with bacon.

BOOK CREDITS & CONTACTS

Brian Basilico, Author

bbasilico@B2b-im.com
www.b2b-im.com
Book Website: www.notaboutu.com

Susan Price, Editor

spricedit@hotmail.com
www.startingyourstory.wordpress.com

Matt Brennan, Author Bio

mattbrennan1980@gmail.com
www.matthewlbrennan.com

Jackson Price, Book Cover & Layout Design

jackson@jpcreative.net
www.jpcreative.net

Lisa Price, Index

lprice0308@gmail.com

INDEX

C

W

Y

Z